NINJA

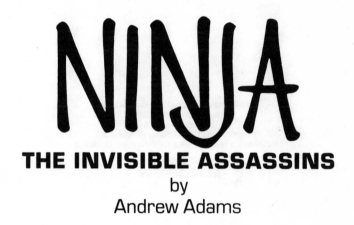

THE INVISIBLE ASSASSINS

by
Andrew Adams

OHARA PUBLICATIONS, INCORPORATED
BURBANK, CALIFORNIA

© 1970 Ohara Publications, Incorporated
Paperback Edition 1973
All rights reserved
Printed in the United States of America
Library of Congress Catalog Card Number 75-136760

Twenty-eighth Printing 1985

ISBN-0-89750-030-X

For Chieko

About the Author

Andrew Morris Adams was born on February 11, 1922 in Glendale, California. After his discharge from the U. S. Navy in 1946, he entered the University of Missouri where his scholastic endeavors were awarded with the inclusion of his name on the Honors List all four years and two degrees: Bachelor of Arts in English Literature and Bachelor of Journalism in Feature Writing. Continuing his education at the University of North Carolina, he was awarded a Master of Arts degree in Dramatic Arts in 1952.

With three specialized degrees in his portfolio, it was no surprise to find Mr. Adams teaching English, journalism and drama at Sullins College in Bristol, Virginia from 1952 until 1956. But his journalistic abilities also took him to the *Arkansas Gazette, Wilmington* (North Carolina) *Star* and the *Bristol Herald-Courier* until 1959 when he went to Japan.

After a few months with the *Pacific Stars & Stripes* and the Kyodo News Agency, Mr. Adams became part of the staff of the *Japan Times* where he still writes sumo commentaries as well as book and drama reviews. For the last few years he has concentrated on free-lance newspaper work, dividing his time between the *Japan Times,* the *San Francisco Chronicle,* the *Daily Mail* and the *Daily Mirror* (London) and CBS News.

Of course, to martial arts fans around the world, the author is perhaps best known for his tremendous contributions to *Black Belt Magazine*. His involved interest in all the martial arts, particularly in judo and sumo, and the obvious intensity of his research into the philosophy of Bushido, have rendered his insight into the mind of the Japanese invaluable to his first book; surely a stunning contribution to the legacy of the ninja.

Acknowledgements

I must first of all give special thanks and acknowledgement to two modern-day ninja practitioners without whose help this book could never have been written. Almost all of the action photographs of ninja demonstrating the use of weapons and special devices as well as unarmed combat have generously been contributed by Yoshiaki Hatsumi of Noda-shi, Chiba-ken. Moreover, his explanations of their uses as well as his comments on ninja training have also been extremely helpful. Hatsumi, who teaches the Togakure School of Ninjitsu, lays claim to being the 34th successor to this school in a direct line of master-student relationships that extend back over a period of seven centuries. He is now writing his own book on Ninjitsu, focusing on ninja techniques.

The other modern ninja whose assistance has been invaluable in the preparation of this book is Heishichiro Okuse, present mayor of Iga-Ueno—former heartland of Ninjitsu—in Mie Prefecture. Regarded as the foremost scholar and historian on the subject, Okuse is also a competent practitioner and occasionally demonstrates ninja techniques at the Ninja Museum in Iga-Ueno. Much of the information contained in the sections on strategy and tactics is based on material from his books. These chapters specifically cover strategy, espionage, tricks, pre-battle tactics, penetration, hiding and escaping as well as history. Okuse has been generous enough to permit use of material from his books **Ninjitsu: Its History and the Ninja**, and **Ninpo: Techniques and Examples**.

Other ninja practitioners who have been helpful in providing me with details about themselves and their own brand of Ninjitsu are Yumio Nawa and Norihiro Iga-Hakuyusai. Nawa was kind enough to demonstrate his manriki-kusari chain techniques. His book, **Ninja Weapons**, was also useful in the preparation of my book. Iga-Hakuyusai, a very busy and elusive present-day ninja, took time out during his rehearsal for a television appearance to talk briefly about himself and the kind of Ninjitsu he demonstrates.

My active and able assistant Nobuo Asahi as well as his predecessor Kazue Itoh were the mediums of the message, diligently interpreting for me at interviews and translating Japanese material into English. Both displayed genuine interest and enthusiasm at all times, even when the project was sputtering along on only a couple of cylinders and threatened more than once to run out of gas short of the goal.

Last, and by far from least, I want to express my heartfelt gratitude to my wife Chieko for her patience, gentle assistance and endless encouragement. Spotting helpful items in the paper or on television, interpreting esoteric telephone conversations from 20th Century ninja and acting as an interpreter at interviews in a pinch are all well-calculated to earn my undying love and gratitude.

Contents

Foreword

Ninjitsu has been variously described as the art of sneaking in, the art of stealth and even the art of invisibility. Actually, none of these definitions really begins to encompass its fantastic boundaries. Simply put, ninja were the cloak-and-dagger artists of Japan's feudal era, from the late 13th Century to the early 17th Century. Like the spectre agents glamorized in the James Bond spy thrillers, ninja involved themselves in everything from espionage, extortion and sabotage to arson, abduction and assassination. They flourished in a period marked by constant upheaval, when rival warlords fought against each other in a ceaseless struggle for power. Although the ninja offered their services to contesting lords, the larger Iga and Koga ninja networks were powers in their own right, dominating the two provinces (now Mie and Shiga Prefectures, respectively) in which they were situated. Here, their schools and networks were set up within their own spheres of influence centered around mighty citadels.

Nearly 2,000 years earlier on the opposite side of the world another power center anticipated much of the rigorous ways followed by these ninja strongholds. Although there is no

THE HEARTLAND OF NINJITSU

THE PULSE OF NINJITSU raced through Central Japan—outlined at right and detailed below—during four centuries of the country's greatest civil strife and turmoil, from 1192-1590. While warlords vied for control of the nation, black-garbed ninja penetrated the country with such advanced espionage techniques as to squeeze the most ironbound of foes. And until the unification of Japan by Hideyoshi Toyotomi in 1590, this rare breed of skilled saboteurs darted from castle towers to marshy waterways throughout Iga and Koga Provinces, creating as much havoc as necessary to effect their lords' aims.

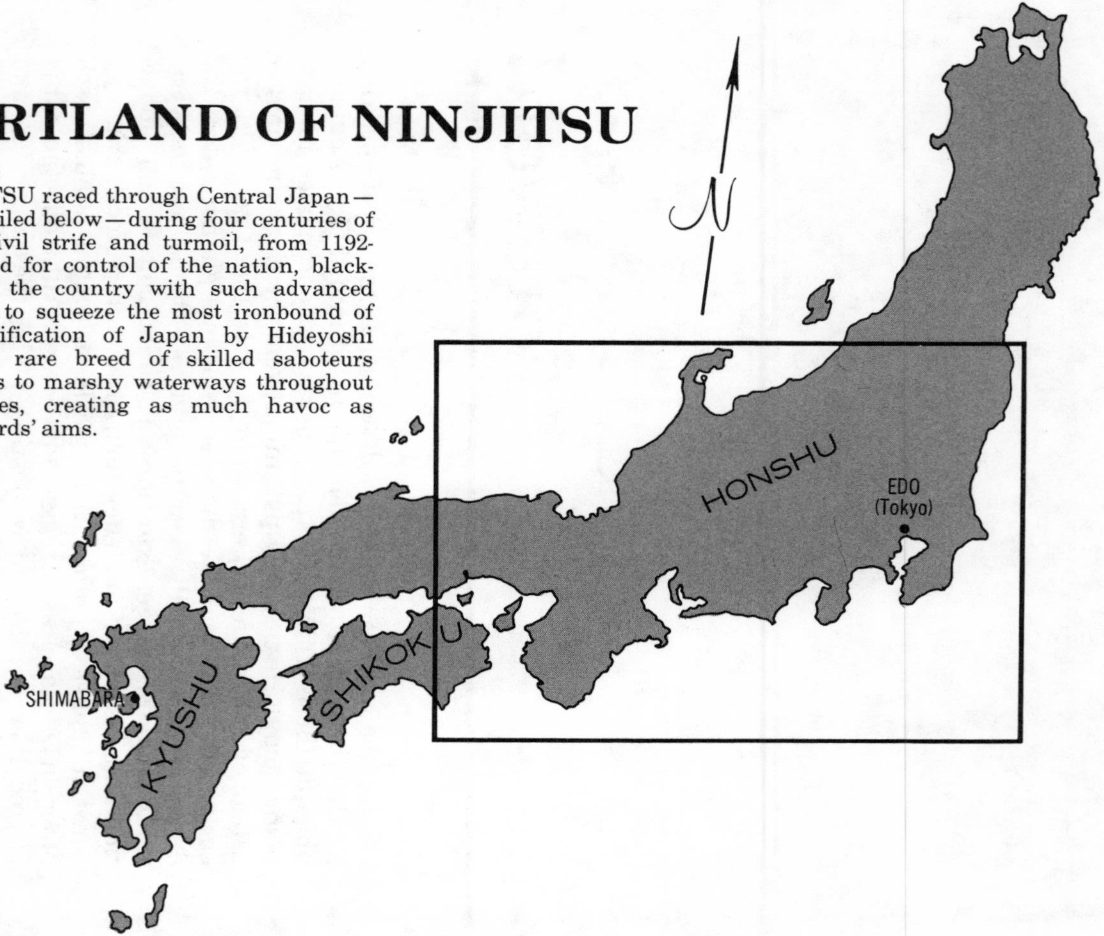

HONSHU

EDO
(Tokyo)

SHIKOKU

KYUSHU

SHIMABARA

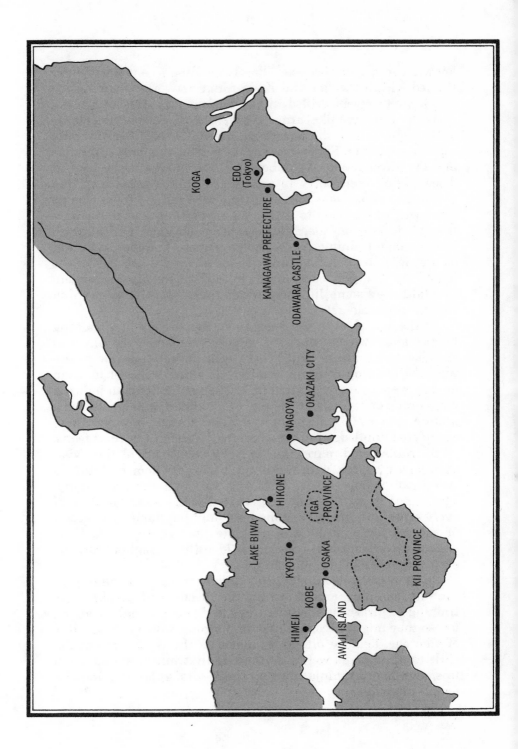

known connection between the two, Japanese youths were trained within the Iga and Koga ninja networks much as the Greek youths were drilled in the ancient city-state of Sparta.

Both were run like armed camps, with Sparta producing only soldiers and the Iga-Koga networks turning out only espionage agents. Spartans were forbidden to engage in trade and the introduction of cumbersome iron money was aimed at discouraging their entry into business. In the same way, Iga and Koga youths were born ninja and died ninja—there was no other way of life open to them. Both Spartans and ninja were thus able to devote their entire time to physical and military or espionage training. Ninja power centers, however, were not so ruthless as the Spartan city-state which got rid of its unhealthy young by exposing them to the elements on a mountain (although some Japanese communities did the same thing to their infirm elders).

At the age of seven the Spartan started undergoing training by the state which consisted almost exclusively of physical exercise and military drill. There was no set time for beginning the training of ninja children; it started almost as soon as they were able to walk and talk. The young Spartan joined a mess group of 15 boys at the age of 20 and was judged to be a mature man at 30. Most Iga and Koga youths, however, were considered full-fledged ninja when they were still in their teens.

Spartans could marry, but only by stealth could they visit their wives; so, too, with the ninja, some of whom maintained two separate households, each with its own wife and family. The life of every Spartan was virtually the same as that of every other and his gravestone bore only his name. The secret of success for a ninja was absolute anonymity. In fact, he went to great lengths to conceal his identity throughout his life, even at times from his fellow-ninja.

Spartan girls also underwent athletic training, engaging in running, jumping and throwing the discus and javelin. The training of girls was instituted not to develop female soldiers, but so they might become brave and strong women, productive of vigorous, healthy offspring, much as the Nazi Herrenvolk. Girls in ninja clans were also thoroughly trained, not so much to spawn healthy ninja boys as to fill vital roles as *kunoichi*, female ninja agents.

The Spartans deliberately set up their self-imposed despotism, a strict form of socialism, which robbed the individual of all freedom and initiative and wiped out the beneficient influences of family life. The ninja also purposefully organized their Spartan way of life, and although it took away their freedom as well, it did not deprive them of initiative. In fact, initiative was especially nourished because when a ninja left on a secret mission, he was pretty much on his own and often only his quick wit kept him alive in times of danger.

The ninja's as well as the Spartan's way of life have continued to appeal to man down through the ages. The story of Sparta, of course, is well-known, but because the incredible ninja are virtually unknown outside Japan, I have undertaken to set down something of their life and times in the fond hope that their story will also prove of interest to people in other parts of the world.

Andrew Adams

FAMED KABUKI ACTOR Danzo Ichikawa presents an imposing re-creation of ninja Niki Danjo weaving one of the secret kuji-kiri finger signs on this ancient scroll from the Edo Period (1616-1867).

22

The Elusive
Phantoms

In all the annals of Japan's long history, no single breed of men ever wreaked more havoc or spawned more terror than the fabulous clans of ninja. Cloaked in black from head to toe and concealing a small arsenal of deadly weapons and secret devices, these medieval masterminds of espionage, sabotage, arson and assassination moved stealthily but relentlessly across the pages of Japan's turbulent era, from the 13th to the 17th Centuries.

Legends even in their own time for their amazing cloak-and-dagger deeds, the ninja were actually capable of performing feats far more fantastic than the mythological marvels accorded them by modern-day films and books. Indeed, the real-life exploits of these sinister bands of espionage experts rival anything ever dreamed up for the fictional super-agent known as James Bond.

Supernatural tales claim the ninja was able to fly, walk on water, live underwater like a fish, become invisible at will, sink into the ground, flow through stone walls, disappear in a puff of smoke and even transform himself into a snake, frog bird or insect. Improbable as these stories may seem, there

23

is a logical explanation for each one, a spark of truth behind the billowing screen of smoke.

The ninja developed the strangest and most chilling art ever to be brought forth from all the vast reaches of Asia. Called *Ninjitsu,* it incorporated the Spartan discipline of Bushido as well as the skills of virtually every martial · art in existence at the time: *kenjitsu* (swordsmanship), *kyujitsu* (skill with the bow and arrow), *yarijitsu* (spear), *bisento* (broadbladed spear), *bojitsu* (stick), *iaijitsu* (fast sword draw), *kusari-gama* (chain and scythe) and *kumi-uchi* (unarmed combat).

The ninja not only had to master all the traditional weapons of the day, but he also had to be skilled at using the awesome collection of special ninja weapons and secret devices including daggers, dirks, darts, star-shaped spurs, medieval brass knuckles, garrotes, caltrops, lead-weighted bamboo staves, rope ladders, grappling hooks, guns, grenades, smoke bombs, eye-blinding powders, acid-spurting tubes and a variety of poisons, to name only a few.

But this was only the beginning of the rugged training for these experts in the not-so-gentle arts of mayhem, counter-intelligence, terrorism and revenge. They practiced muscular control and body movements for endless hours to be able to accomplish fantastic physical feats such as scaling sheer walls and cliffs, staying submerged under water for several minutes at a time, and through reduced breathing techniques, actually appearing to be dead at times to deceive their enemies.

It goes without saying, then, that the ninja was a super-athlete capable of great physical feats. He could walk and run faster and further than ordinary men, jump higher and further, swim faster and longer, fast for days and endure tremendous hardships. Seiko Fujita, a ninja descendant who died a few years ago, claimed that ninja could jump over seven feet and walk the 350 miles between Tokyo and Osaka in only three days.

Of necessity, the ninja was a superb escape artist who would have made Houdini look like a rank amateur. He could dislocate his joints at will to slip out of the most complicated knots. He hid in bells, above ceilings, under floors, remained submerged under water by breathing through reeds and tobacco pipes, concealed himself in trees and wells and even disguised himself as a rock or tree stump. In fact, his ability to appear unobtrusive and disappear into the surrounding scenery was what probably gave rise to tales that ninja could make themselves invisible at will. It should come as no surprise, then, that Ninjitsu has been defined as the "Art of Invisibility".

In many ways ninja bore a remarkable resemblance to American Indians. Stoical by nature and Spartan in their habits, both breeds developed great strength and endurance. They both learned to walk noiselessly and cover long distances in an amazingly short span of time. They could also detect the sound of approaching danger by putting one ear to the ground. Both were not only excellent horsemen, but were also skilled with a knife as well as bow and arrow. The ninja as well as the American Indian used flaming arrows to set enemy camps on fire and communicated with smoke signals by day, animal and bird calls by night. They prided themselves on their personal courage, preferring death to surrender or capture.

The ninja was also a consumate actor and a master of disguises, the original man of a thousand faces. Contrary to the filmland image of the ninja as a black-costumed character, slinking about castle walls at night, he was a steel-nerved spy who might appear as a priest one day, a carpenter the next and an enemy soldier on the third day.

But he didn't merely play the part of a carpenter or priest; he had to know practically all there was to know about the profession he assumed. And when he moved into a new community on a special mission, he was thoroughly schooled in the geography, manners, customs and dialect of that region as well as the personal backgrounds of the leading dignitaries living there.

Of course, the most exciting missions were carried out at night, preferably on moonless or stormy nights when the black-clothed ninja was virtually invisible. In winter when snow covered the ground he donned an all-white uniform. Even his sword scabbard was white and on his white *tabi* (split-toed shoe socks) and straw sandals he tied a five-bladed

25

CLOAKING HIS PRESENCE against a tree, a ninja blends in with the foliage so effectively it is almost impossible to detect him. The ninja's ability to merge with the surrounding scenery was uncanny.

26

WINTERTIME CAMOUFLAGE includes an all-white uniform. The ninja wears white tabi with blades tied onto the bottom to walk on hard ice.

DISGUISED AS A PRIEST, a ninja defends himself with a bo against his sword-wielding foe who is dressed in traditional ninja wear.

metal device that enabled him to walk easily over hard snow and ice.

On long missions, the ninja carried highly concentrated food and drink, a sort of feudal-age K-rations. A proficient pharmacist, the ninja concocted his own lethal store of poisons as well as his own supply of medicines and curatives, explosives and blinding powders, energy foods and pep drinks. When wounded or sick, he was often his own doctor and prescribed his own cures.

The ninja might be sent out to steal information, track enemy movements or, through trickery, attempt to mislead the enemy about the intentions of his lord's army. And if that didn't suffice, he might be called on to sneak into the enemy camp and commit arson, sabotage or even assassinate the opposing warlord. Divided into three ranks, leaders, sub-leaders and ordinary agents, the large networks of ninja sometimes had 1,000 or more men.

These networks of spies also included female ninja called *kunoichi*. A feudal-age Mata Hari was often a ravishing beauty plucked from among the ninja clans or recruited from sympathetic families in enemy country. Her main task was to use her feminine charms to draw vital secrets from enemy leaders. Although she was taught to handle ninja weapons, her main assassination tool was a long, lethal-looking hairpin innocently concealed in her coiffure.

A man was born a ninja and died a ninja. There were few outsiders among the ninja clans that flourished in the Iga and Koga Provinces north of Kyoto and Nara and southwest of Nagoya in the rugged, hilly country of central Japan. One network of ninja agents might be employed by a local lord seeking to free his subjects from oppression, while another band would bind themselves to an ambitious *daimyo* (a feudal lord) trying to expand his lands and power.

The secret of staying alive for a ninja was to remain anonymous, and only a few masters achieved any sort of renown. Ninja traitors were ruthlessly hunted down and killed by fellow ninja. If one were on the verge of being captured, he invariably killed himself to prevent the enemy from torturing vital secrets out of him. Some were known to have dislocated their jaws to keep from talking, while others slashed their faces to ribbons with a knife to prevent identification. Since ninja often worked in teams, accompanying ninja sometimes slew their cohorts when the latter were on the point of being taken to keep them from confessing vital secrets under torture. A poison-tipped dirk or dart was usually all that was necessary.

One of the most intriguing aspects of Ninjitsu was the use of magical in-signs made with the fingers called *kuji-kiri*. The idea was to fix the enemy with a weird knitting of the fingers, a hypnotic stare and strange chanting in order to confuse and disconcert him. At the same time it served to restore the ninja's self-confidence and enable him to concentrate all his energy and will power on overcoming desperate situations. A sort of feudal-age hex, it could sometimes perplex the enemy just long enough to allow the ninja to escape.

The unification of Japan marked the abrupt end to ninja activities, except in support of the state. Further internecine warfare among rival warlords or against the state was strictly prohibited and drastic measures were taken to enforce this ban by requiring either the lord or members of his family to remain as hostages on alternate years in the shogun's castle in Edo. This also meant the outlawing of ninja networks to prevent their conspiring against the shogun. The henchmen of local lords often disguised themselves in black ninja garb in making nighttime forays against one another. However, these bodyguards and samurai retainers were ninja in appearance only and indeed gave Ninjitsu a bad name since not a few of them were gangsters, outlaws and oppressors.

When in the 17th Century the Tokugawa Shogun banned the practice of Ninjitsu or even mention of the subject on penalty of death, it set a seal of secrecy on the occult art that has persisted to the present day. Through the years, only a handful of men continued to practice as ninja to keep alive at least the less lethal traditions of the art. On a chance, a Japanese film company produced a low-budget movie a few years ago about the ancient exploits of the ninja, based on a scientific approach to the subject. Even the film promoters were astonished when they ended up with a full-scale hit on their hands.

NINJA

A flood of interest followed. Books, films, television serials, magazines, exhibitions and demonstrations came pouring out in bewildering fashion. Before long, the half dozen or so formerly obscure practitioners of the art suddenly found themselves lionized and written about in the press. The ninja craze even spread to Australia where enthusiastic young fans recently mobbed a Japanese actor playing the title role in a ninja television series called "Samurai" dubbed into English and viewed by Australian audiences.

The recent attempt by a self-styled ninja to slip into the former Imperial Palace in Kyoto, 320 miles southwest of Tokyo, marked another incident in the current revival of interest in Ninjitsu. Clothed in black from head to foot with a typical ninja uniform that included a mask and metal wrist bands, the youthful cloak-and-dagger artist fled over the stone wall after a guard spotted him crouching in the darkness. At the end of a hot chase, however, he was humiliatingly captured. When searched, the 16-year-old intruder coughed up a regular arsenal of lethal weapons: 12 steel darts, fireworks, a straw rope with a hook attached, a knife and gunpowder. He explained that he broke into the heavily-guarded palace because it was a good place to test his technique.

But this amateurish attempt was a far cry from the original ninja who could sneak undetected into the most strongly-protected castles and strongholds. The would-be ninja's forebear took great pride in his secret abilities which were passed on from father to son, from master to student. Books and documents on Ninjitsu were closely guarded as family treasures, never being allowed outside the house. Perhaps this is why there are only a handful of authentic practitioners of Ninjitsu remaining today. The rest are all outsiders.

Shadows
of the Past

Ninjitsu is supposed to have originated more than 2,000 years ago as a treatise on the art of spying in the ancient Chinese book on military science called *Sun Tzu*. It was written by the great Chinese strategist Sun Wu who lived between 500 and 300 B.C.

But it wasn't until the 6th Century A.D. that spy tactics were introduced into Japan. Prince Regent Shotoku (593-622 A.D.) first employed agents to secretly probe both sides in civil suits to get at the truth of a dispute. For the next 500 years or so Ninjitsu gradually developed through the efforts of such groups as the rebellious mountain priests known as *Yamabushi* (literally, "mountain warriors").

After the death of Prince Shotoku, the Japanese became embroiled in a bitter power struggle between the Buddhists and Shintoists over which doctrine would be designated as the state religion. The struggle soon involved influential court nobles, throwing the nation into disorder. At this point a Yamabushi named En-no-Gyoja appeared on the scene and tried to restore order with *Shugendo*, a new way of propagating Buddhism.

31

As the new religious campaign gained increasing support from the people, it was inevitable that the aristocracy would force a showdown with En-no-Gyoja and his followers. Obviously fearing that the Yamabushi would gain ruling power, the nobles sent large government forces to subdue them. Forced to fight against great odds, these rugged warrior priests borrowed Chinese military tactics and strategy for use in both individual combat and collective fighting.

The incorporation of *Omyodo* in the Heian Period (794-1185) marked another big step forward for Ninjitsu. Omyodo, an ancient synthetic science which includes the Chinese art of divination and the science of astrology, was widely practiced by the Yamabushi and other warriors. The powerful Genji Clan which ruled Japan at this time along with the rival Heike Clan maintained close ties with the Yamabushi forerunners of ninja. Ninjitsu was included among the martial arts which the Genji warriors were required to master in carrying out the imperial command to suppress the Ainu and other rebels along the frontiers, much as the U. S. government dispatched the cavalry after the Civil War to quell the Indian "rebels" in the West.

Despite these developments it was the middle of the Heian Period before Ninjitsu took firm root and assumed the basic form that it was to follow over the next four centuries. Iga Province (now Mie Prefecture) came under the control of the Hattori Clan whose members were taught the art of espionage by the ascetics and Yamabushi living in the province. And it was here that the Hattori family established the basis of the Iga School of Ninjitsu.

Surprise Attack

At the end of the period in 1185 the central government in Kyoto had become so weak that the capital was ruled at night by three robbers who had learned Ninjitsu from the Yamabushi of Mt. Kurama, north of the capital. Various budo schools were set up at this time to train budding young warriors and secret agents, including one famous ninja school established by the famous Genji warrior-hero Yoshitsune. The oldest Ninjitsu school in Japan, it stressed

TO CONFUSE HIS ENEMIES and conceal his identity, famed ninja Sandayu Momochi maintained three separate residences with a different wife and family living at each one such as his home (above) in the Oka-One mountain range of Nabari. Below is a glimpse of the wild, hilly country where the Iga ninja flourished during the 16th Century.

WINGED, LONG-NOSED GOBLINS called tengu are the legendary, original ninja from whom all ninja are said to have sprung.

FAMED NINJA LEADER Hanzo Hattori, left, served as a special espionage agent to military general Ieyasu Tokugawa, center, who later established the 250-year-long Tokugawa Shogunate dynasty. At right is war lord Hideyoshi Toyotomi who helped to unite Japan in the late 16th Century.

jumping and the strategy of surprise attack, a sinister strategy that centuries later reached near-perfection in the disastrous surprise attacks against the Chinese in 1895, the Russians at Port Arthur in 1904 and the Americans at Pearl Harbor in 1941.

Before setting up his own Ninjitsu school, Yoshitsune had mastered martial arts taught at the Kurama-Hachi-ryu School which had been organized by the Yamabushi of Mt. Kurama. But neither the Kurama establishment nor that of the Yoshitsune-ryu meant that Ninjitsu had finally become an independent art. On the contrary, it continued to be taught merely as one of the collective martial arts. In fact it was not until the flowering of the Hattori and Momochi Clans during the late 12th Century in Iga Province, the cradle of Ninjitsu, that the art eventually came into its own.

The rise of the samurai and the shogunate style of government in the Kamakura Period (1192-1333) marked the beginning of the "Golden Age of Ninjitsu" that would eventually spread over the following four centuries. Some 25 different schools sprang up during this period with the strongholds of the art concentrated in the Iga and Koga Provinces. Zen was introduced into Japan about this time and laid the basis for samurai culture. The Hattori and Oe Clans jointly ruled Iga Province, while in Koga Province to the north more than 50 Ninjitsu families provided the foundation for the Koga School of Ninjitsu.

Another early Ninjitsu school, Kusunoki-ryu, was set up in the mid-14th Century by a famous warrior named Masahige Kusunoki. Although both schools made good use of the surprise attack, the earlier Yoshitsune-ryu stressed direct fighting methods, while the Kusunoki-ryu concentrated on spying activities through an extensive intelligence network. Kusunoki based his operations on a ring of 48 Iga ninja agents stationed in the cities of Kyoto, Osaka and Kobe where they collected information on hostile movements by the enemy.

Somewhat resembling the struggle between the United States' northern and southern states some 500 years later, Japan was also torn by a bitter civil war in the 14th Century

"TANBA NO KAMI", a title of nobility by which Iga ninja leader Sandayu Momochi was also known, marks the site of his main stronghold. This mountain fastness was razed by Nobunaga Oda in 1581.

THE 17TH DESCENDENT of Sandayu Momochi, Itsuki Momochi, lives in the 400-year-old farmhouse of his daring forebear, in the mountains about 15 miles south of Iga-Ueno in Nabari. Below, the Momochi family graveyard where the renowned ninja master lies buried is now overgrown with weeds.

between the northern and southern dynasties. And like the American struggle, the North won out when the warring sides were unified by the northern emperor in 1392. But around the middle of the next century some 75 years later, more civil strife erupted. Things went from bad to worse and the entire country was virtually ripped apart by one struggle after another until Hideyoshi Toyotomi united Japan in 1590.

But it was during those four centuries of civil war and ceaseless power struggles that the ninja were in greatest demand by ambitious warlords. Although many schools of Ninjitsu flourished at this time, none could rival the traditional Koga and Iga schools for technical excellence.

Portuguese traders brought guns – firelocks – into Japan in 1543, and although their use somewhat modified traditional strategy, it was not until the Imperial Restoration in 1868 and the Satsuma Rebellion a decade later that guns played a decisive role in military encounters.

Even the use of guns and gunpowder did not basically alter the traditional methods of espionage employed by the ninja. It merely added variety to their arsenal and diversified their strategy. About the only way in which ninja made use of fire before the advent of gunpowder was to relay information by lighting signal fires on mountain tops like the American Indians with their smoke signalling. They also made use of various kinds of torches.

But now the ninja devised smoke grenades to create smoke screens, made pocket-sized guns for assassinations and even developed explosive arrows, land mines and wooden cannons. Some of the latter were small enough to be fired while held in the arms like a bazooka.

Many of the warlords of the time hired ninja to spy on each other's movements. Two of the more well-known leaders were Shingen Takeda and his long-time rival Kenshin Uesugi. Takeda's ninja agents set up relays of signal fires on mountain tops to flash information from the imperial capital of Kyoto to his mountain stronghold, while Uesugi's spies conducted their activities by disguising themselves as medicine peddlers. Ieyasu Tokugawa, the illustrious general who later established a family dynasty of shoguns that was to last for two-and-a-half centuries, also employed Iga and Koga ninja who frequently carried out surprise attacks against the enemy during battles.

Although Koga Province was ruled by more than 50 ninja clans, only three old families held sway in Iga Province: the Hattoris, the Momochis and the Fujibayashis. The Momochi Clan governed the southern part of the province, the Hattoris the central section and the Fujibayashi family the northern half as well as the southern part of Koga Province, thus utilizing both Iga and Koga ninja in its network.

Three of the most famous ninja leaders in history were Sandayu Momochi, Hanzo Hattori and Nagato Fujibayashi, all three of whom operated in the Iga region during the stormy 16th Century. In order to confuse his enemies and conceal his identity, Sandayu maintained three separate houses with a separate wife and family living at each one. When things got too hot in one area, he would change houses and assume a different identity. One of his most well-known ninja henchmen was a man named Goemon Ishikawa who later became a notorious robber. Goemon was finally caught and given the terrible sentence of being boiled to death in a huge cauldron of hot, bubbling water.

Foes of Buddhism

There were three distinguished warlords living at that time: Nobunaga Oda and his two generals, Hideyoshi Toyotomi and Ieyasu Tokugawa. Oda and Toyotomi used many military spies, but none of them were Iga or Koga ninja. Since Ninjitsu developed from the Yamabushi, it was only natural that the ninja continued to maintain close ties with Buddhist leaders. Oda and Toyotomi, on the other hand, were the relentless foes of Buddhism, suppressing priests and burning their temples at every opportunity. Thus, the Iga and Koga ninja became the sworn enemies of these great warlords.

This enmity plus a series of futile attempts by ninja to assassinate Gen. Oda led this ruthless leader on November 3, 1581, to invade Iga Province with his 46,000-man army and attack a combined force of Iga ninja of less than 4,000

THE 400-YEAR-OLD FARMHOUSE once occupied by Sandayu Momochi is the setting for a family portrait of Itsuki Momochi's wife and three children.

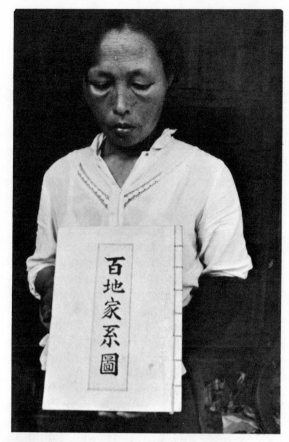

THE FAMILY TREE is carefully displayed by Mrs. Momochi. These documents are among the few remaining treasures uniting the 20th Century farmer with the 16th Century exploits of the glorious ninja leader.

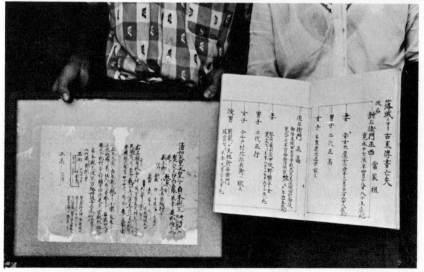

41

men. In little less than a week Nobunaga Oda had brought the area under his iron fist, after slaying large numbers of ninja and executing most of those he captured. The survivors fled the province and scattered to every part of the country, later serving other warlords.

According to a chronicle of the battle, Sandayu Momochi fought with courage and gallantry in combat, but there is no mention of Nagato Fujibayashi. From this omission several historians have concluded that these two personages were in fact one and the same person using different disguises. Two of Sandayu's houses are still standing today. The third, the main stronghold in the hills around Iga-Ueno called Takiguchi-jo, was razed by Oda. Since Sandayu's death was never confirmed, it is believed he may have escaped during the battle, fled to the east and settled down in Kii Province disguised as a farmer. This is all the more plausible since this province was beyond Oda's sphere of influence and dominated by several clans of militant Buddhists.

Sandayu continued to give history the slip for almost four centuries. But modern science finally caught up with the elusive ninja. Only a few years ago a graves expert located his grave. It was found in a small family plot on a hill opposite one of his former houses in the hills behind Nabari, about 15 miles south of Iga-Ueno. Apparently, the ninja leader managed to make his way back to his home country before he died. The secret paths behind these houses which Sandayu used to slip from one to another can still be seen.

The 17th descendant of Sandayu Momochi still lives in the 400-year-old farm house at the northern foot of the Oka-One mountain range with his wife and three children. He is Itsuke Momochi, a 58-year-old farmer. But Itsuki is far more interested in crops than dead ninja, and he has only a family document to show for the Momochi family's rich ninja heritage. It seems his grandfather rounded up most of the family's ninja relics and sold them to museums and private collectors in Tokyo many years ago.

On a high hill overlooking the city of Iga-Ueno, the

heartland of Ninjitsu, is the towering Hakuho (White Phoenix) Castle. It was built in the 16th Century by feudal lord Takatora Toda who gathered many ninja to his fold and helped train them. The prototype of the castle of Edo (now Tokyo), the Hakuho Castle has a deep well leading to a tunnel which was used as an emergency escape route. The castle was severely damaged by a typhoon a few years ago, but was recently restored to its original glory.

The Koga ninja were also centered around a castle town to the north. And like the White Phoenix Castle of Iga-Ueno, the imposing castle at Hikone on the east banks of Lake Biwa in what is now Shiga Prefecture is also still standing. Moreover, many of the neighborhoods in these two towns still carry the names of the ninja families who once lived there such as Iga-cho and Shinobi-cho. Some historians claim that the Koga ninja are descended from *ronin* (masterless samurai) who settled in the area and organized themselves as rivals of the Iga ninja.

Less than a year after Nobunaga Oda razed the homes and strongholds of the Iga ninja clans, the famed warlord himself was dead, killed in Kyoto at the hands of a rival warlord, once his own staff colonel, by the name of Mitsuhide Akechi. At the time, one of Oda's leading generals, Ieyasu Tokugawa, was in a small town near Osaka called Sakai and in danger of being attacked by Akechi's soldiers. Fortunately, Tokugawa was able to obtain the services of the surviving Iga ninja leader Hanzo Hattori and his followers to serve as bodyguards for the general on his return to his headquarters at Okazaki.

Hattori's protection was so effective that Tokugawa made him and his men his personal retainers, later incorporating them into his secret service network when he became *Shogun* (military dictator). Hattori was designated as the chief, with his Iga ninja followers given the posts of "gardeners" around the Shogun's quarters in the Edo Castle compound. Although actually serving as bodyguards to the Shogun, they performed regular gardening work during normal times. But when an emergency arose they were personally assigned to intelligence missions, while the Shogun's Koga ninja cohorts were appointed as police sergeants.

THE HEARTLAND OF NINJITSU—the valley of Iga-Ueno—is shown on this Hiroshige woodblock print from the Edo Period. In the distance is the famed Hakuho (White Phoenix) Castle.

RISING ABOVE THE TREES on a hill overlooking Iga-Ueno is the Hakuho Castle. Built in the 1500s by Takatora Toda, the castle was recently restored after having been destroyed by a typhoon a few years ago.

A VIEW OF IGA-UENO is seen today from the Hakuho Castle where centuries ago feudal lord Toda gathered ninja to his fold. In one part of the castle is a deep well used as an emergency escape route.

NINJA

The Shogun often sent out his ninja agents to investigate the activities of his restless vassal daimyo since they were constantly threatening to revolt. The feudal lords, needless to say, were always on the alert for these ninja agents and ordered them secretly liquidated whenever their identities were discovered. The powerful Satsuma Clan which ruled southern Kyushu almost like a separate nation was so wary that it was said nine out of ten ninja sent into that province never returned.

Police Force

The last major military role played by the Iga ninja was the key part 10 ninja performed in leading the Tokugawa Shogun's army to victory over some 40,000 rebellious Christians holed up in a castle in Shimabara, Kyushu, in 1637. As peace and order were restored to the nation and their services as political intelligence agents were no longer required, many ninja were put to work as policemen and detectives. Some of the Iga ninja, however, remained "gardeners" for the Shogun.

Permanent peace also forced the ninja to switch from their specialized espionage training to the development of their skills as criminal investigators. At the beginning of the 18th Century the former Iga and Koga ninja making up the Edo police force were reinforced by ninja from other areas, including Negoro-ryu ninja, followers from a branch of the Iga School of Ninjitsu. The descendants of these ninja-turned-detectives also played a vital role as policemen, even after the collapse of the shogunate government in 1867.

The Iga ninja had perhaps the most effective intelligence network for carrying out their police activities. After their defeat by Nobunaga Oda in 1581, they escaped by scattering to the four corners of the country. Moreover, their descendants continued to live in their new hometowns where they also turned to police work. Thus, it was a simple matter for these Iga ninja-police to form a nationwide network among the members of their own clan for the exchange of information and the tracking of criminals.

While some ninja enforced the law, other down-and-out

ninja broke it. Becoming robbers and thieves was an easy transition for them. Goemon Ishikawa, one of Sandayu Momochi's leading lieutenants, was perhaps the most disreputable of those who chose this way of life although many Japanese regard him as a loveable rogue – a sort of Robin Hood of Japan. Even down to the present, the lure of ninja tactics persists among thieves. A few years ago police in Tokyo's neighboring Kanagawa Prefecture rounded up a gang of 10 young "ninja" sneak thieves. Dressing themselves in the traditional black garb of the ninja, they even broke into a golf clubhouse run by the U. S. Navy.

Today, hardly more than half a dozen ninja practitioners are still active in carrying on the traditions of their forebears. Restrictive laws also require them to concentrate on unarmed methods of self-defense for the most part. Thus, Ninjitsu continues to be kept alive at present only by a handful of dedicated men.

Weapons

The ninja was required to master the most awesome array of weapons ever assembled at any one period in history. They included not only such traditional arms as the sword, spear, bisento, stick, bow and arrow, but also dirks, daggers, darts caltrops, guns, explosives, blinders, poisons and so on. In addition, he was adept in the art of unarmed combat.

Even when the ninja employed orthodox arms, he often used them in unorthodox ways. The sword he carried was equipped with an oversized guard which he used as a sort of step or hook to help him climb or pull himself up over obstacles. His skill as an archer came in handy when he wanted to set fire to a structure Indian-style by means of a flaming arrow. When he carried a spear, he sometimes converted it into a kind of vaulting pole. Even the sword scabbard could be useful to a ninja. The tip could be removed to permit the ninja to use the scabbard as a hearing aid, a megaphone or an underwater breathing tube.

The ninja also used the sheath, or scabbard, in defending himself against a spear attack or probing for sleeping enemies in a pitch-dark room. In the first case, the ninja

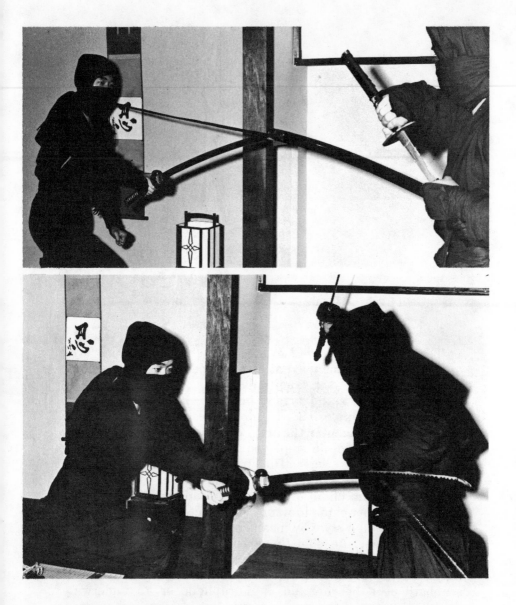

PROBING FOR HIS ENEMY in a dark room, a ninja, at left, balances the scabbard on the tip of his sword with a cord extending from his teeth to the sheath. The touch of the scabbard awakens the sleeping victim who prepares to draw his own sword. Below, the ninja quickly releases the cord, then strikes with his unsheathed sword.

50

SEEMINGLY INNOCENT-LOOKING, this bamboo staff, or shinobi-zue, was really a deadly weapon. A long knife inserted at one end could be flashed out with a quick flip of the wrist. Below, a ninja uses the chain and weight at one end to pull an enemy off his feet. He then quickly moves in and slams the opposite end of the staff—weighted with lead—against his foe's head.

would hold up the scabbard with his left hand and the sword in his right, with a cord connecting the two pieces at their base. Then, when the spearman lunged forward, the ninja would move slightly to the left and allow the spear to pass under his right arm. And before his opponent could withdraw his spear, the ninja quickly wrapped the cord around it, spun his opponent around and struck him down from behind with his sword before the spearman could draw his own sword.

When a ninja found himself in a room where it was too dark to see, he could not afford to move around for fear of stumbling over a sleeping enemy and thus raising an alarm. Instead, he balanced his scabbard on the tip of his sword, with a cord extending from the scabbard opening and held between his teeth. The scabbard could thus be used to lightly probe for sleeping figures. If the sleeping person awakened and jumped up, preparing to draw his own sword, the ninja quickly dropped the scabbard by releasing the cord from between his teeth and struck down his enemy first with his unsheathed sword. Moreover, the ninja had the advantage of knowing just about where his enemy was despite the darkness, thanks to the slight contact made by the scabbard. His just-awakened opponent, on the other hand, would have no clear idea in which direction he should attack.

According to a ninja practitioner living in Tokyo named Yumio Nawa, the sword was the ninja's most important weapon. They used a shorter blade than usual, not longer than 20 inches, for better mobility. Another modern-day ninja, Yoshiaki Hatsumi, teaches the art of wielding the *bisento,* a spear-like weapon with a blade at the end that resembles a scimitar.

The ninja also learned to handle the *bo,* or stick, another of the traditional weapons around which a martial art, *bojitsu,* developed. Here, again, he turned it into a much more versatile weapon than it was originally intended for. An innocent-looking bamboo staff carried by a seemingly helpless priest often proved to be a powerful weapon (*shinobi-zue*) wielded by a well-trained ninja.

Attacked by a swordsman, the ninja would bend low, quickly remove the metal cap at the end and sweep the staff a foot or so above the ground. Out whipped a six-foot-long chain with a

HURLING the ring end of a kyoketsu-shogi at his opponent's arms, Hatsumi forces him to drop his sword, pulls him in close, and goes to work with the double-pointed knife at the other end of his weapon.

FOUR SHARP SPIKES protrude from the under, or palm side, of the tekagi, a sort of feudal-age brass knuckles. Below, Yoshiaki Hatsumi demonstrates the use of this fearsome weapon in besting a swordsman. Blocking the sword blow with his tekagi-protected left hand, Hatsumi deals a vicious blow with his right hand against his opponent's head.

weight on the end that immediately wrapped itself around the attacker's leg. And before his enemy could retaliate, the ninja would jerk him forward off-balance to the ground, then quickly move in and slam the opposite end of the staff, which just happened to be weighted with lead, against his foe's head. End of battle.

Some staves were weighted at one end and carried a small feathered dart, dirk or lead balls at the other, open end. Presumably going on the defensive by bracing himself for a sword attack, the ninja would suddenly flick his staff forward and, aiming at his enemy's eyes, let the missile fly. If his adversary were able to duck out of the way in time, the ninja would dash forward and clobber him on the back of the head with the weighted end before he could see the attack coming.

Blindman's Bluff

Other staves had a long, sharp knife at the open end which could be flipped out with a quick wrist motion, converting the staff into a kind of spear. A blind man probing his way with a cane might suddenly swing his cane forward so sharply a sword blade would flash out at the end. Opening his eyes, he would go into action as a well-armed ninja with his trusty *shikomi-zue*.

Ninja made use of other dual-purpose weapons, such as *kusari-gama* and *kyoketsu-shogi*. Although a martial art has also grown up around kusari-gama, it differs from the traditional martial arts in that it was not developed by the samurai, but by farmers as a means of defending themselves against robbers and marauding ronin. Consisting of a hand scythe and a length of chain with an iron ball or weight at the end, it was also practiced as a supplement to jujitsu in later years much as the tonfa was incorporated with karate.

The scythe and chain were especially effective against the sword, the scythe being used both to block the striking sword as well as to deal a slashing counterattack against a vital part of the head, neck or torso. The ninja could wrap the chain around the neck or an arm to pinion the latter out of harm's way as well as use the chain to block the sword. The iron ball or weight was usually wielded in a counter-attacking

逃走の武器 ── ひし

忍者は、ひしを撒いて逃走した ── すなはち追はれた時、敵を狭い通路に導き、いきなりひしを撒く。── 敵はそのひしを踏んで倒れ ── 戦斗力を失うというダンドリである。

ひしには次の三つがある。

A FAVORITE TRICK to slow down the enemy when a ninja was being hotly pursued was to strew a handful of multi-pointed tetsu-bishi, or caltrops, behind him, such as those shown above and at right. Natural plant caltrops, below, could be nearly as painful as the steel points.

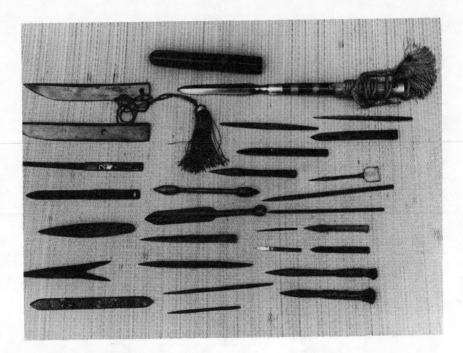

DEFENSE WEAPONS included small metal weapons such as dirks, darts and shuriken which could be thrown at the enemy when the ninja was spotted and attacked or when he was escaping from pursuers. Collectively known as tonki, the little weapons were stuffed into the ninja's pouch and pockets whenever he started out on a secret mission.

NINJA PRACTICED continually until they could practically hit a dime with these little shuriken and dirks, until accurate aiming and throwing became second nature. Held between the thumb and forefinger, shuriken, at right, were tossed overhead as well as side-arm. The dirks, above, were held in the palm of the hand and thrown side-arm, underhand and overhand.

blow against the temple or other part of the head.

Holding the scythe in his right hand and the iron ball in his left, the ninja traditionally blocked his enemy's attack by catching the sword blade in the joint of the kama. From that crucial stage he could either close in quickly and strike his foe in the head with the iron weight, or pivot to one side, seize his opponent's right wrist and then reach over with the scythe and rip open the left side of his neck.

Another potent weapon that was a favorite with ninja was the *kyoketsu-shogi*. Attached to one end of a cord which was often made of women's hair for extra strength was a metal ring and at the other end a vicious-looking, double-pointed knife. The ring end of the cord was thrown and wrapped around an opponent's arm or neck, after which the ninja pulled him in close. He then cut down sharply with the curved knife edge across the enemy's neck and followed through with the straight knife by thrusting upward into a vital spot such as the bowels, stomach or chest. The ring could also be tossed around one leg so the ninja could pull his attacker off-balance and spring on him with the knife-end of the kyoketsu-shogi.

Tiger's Claws

One fierce little weapon used by Hatsumi's Togakure School of Ninjitsu is called a *shuko,* or *tekagi.* A sort of feudal-age brass knuckles, it was made of one narrow and one wide metal band joined by a flat metal section. The narrow band slipped over the hand and tightened around the wrist, leaving the wide band to encircle the hand. From the under, or palm side, of the wide band protruded four sharp spikes.

The tekagi was another dual-purpose weapon, useful for gripping when climbing walls, pillars, trees and cliffs. But more importantly, a sudden swipe with it could prove to be more deadly than a swat by an angry tiger. Fighting at close quarters, the ninja could block a sword swipe and rake an enemy's face with the spikes on the palm side or break his jaw with a blow from the back of the metal band.

Whenever a ninja started out on a secret mission, he invariably stuffed his pouch with plenty of *tonki,* a whole class of small metal weapons used primarily for escape tactics. The tonki consisted of an astonishing assortment of dirks, daggers, darts and various other pointed weapons.

Tonki also included a particularly vicious little item called *tetsu-bishi*. When the ninja were being hotly pursued, one of their favorite tricks to slow down the enemy was to strew a handful of four-pointed tetsu-bishi behind them. Known as caltrops in the West, they were designed so that no matter which way they landed, one sharp point always protruded straight up. Since Japanese in those days usually wore straw sandals, one misstep on a tetsu-bishi was usually enough to persuade a pursuer to give up the chase. These caltrops were also spread around an encampment or along castle walls and approaches to prevent enemy ninja spies from sneaking undetected past the guards. It would be pretty hard to stifle a howl of pain after suddenly stepping on one of these little sharp-pointed beauties. Apparently, they even find use today, for "007" in one of his early adventures, "Casino Royale", tosses out a handful of caltrops to discourage a car from following him.

Multi-pointed throwing weapons called *shuriken* were an indispensable part of the tonki arsenal used by the ninja. These consisted of little, hand-thrown weapons with anywhere from three to 10 points. Altogether there were 10 different kinds of shuriken, depending on the shape. They were cross-shaped, triangular, four-pointed, star-shaped, six-pointed, eight-pointed, 10-pointed and swastica-shaped. In addition, there were many variations of the latter.

The multi-pointed shuriken of which the four-pointed and star-shaped variety were the most popular were held between the thumb and forefinger and tossed overhand or sidearm with a quick, spinning motion. They were mostly nuisance weapons, aimed at the eyes, temple, brow, throat or heart. In this way they were designed to stop pursuers only momentarily, or by striking one of their arms or hands they could prevent opponents from effectively wielding a sword. Ninja constantly practiced hurling the small shuriken at tree trunks, posts and other fixed targets until they could practically hit a dime with them. As a result, accurate aiming and swift throwing eventually became instinctive to the ninja, although the effective range was limited to about 30 feet.

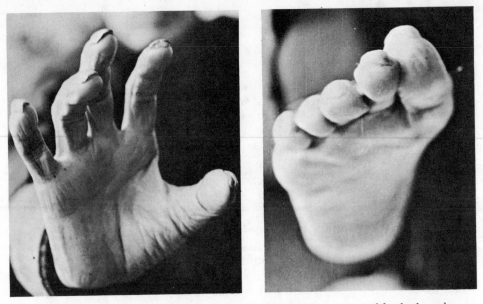

METAL CLAWS, attached to fingernails and toenails, were used by both male and female ninja. As sharp as needles, the claws could easily penetrate the most vital parts of the human body.

BLOWGUNS shot poisoned darts and pins, called fukiya, with deadly accuracy, even against fellow-ninja on the point of capture to prevent them from being tortured into revealing secret plans or the identities of their cohorts.

POISON-WATER GUNS, demonstrated by Yoshiaki Hatsumi, were designed to blind the eyes of an enemy within a range of about 60 feet.

SMOKE BOMBS were used to screen the ninja's activities. Smoke grenades, such as the one Hatsumi holds, were also used for signaling.

The more lethal tonki were tipped with poison. Like jungle tribes around the world, the ninja also shot pins and poisoned darts called *fukiya* through blowguns with deadly accuracy, even against fellow-ninja on the point of being captured to prevent them from being tortured into revealing secret plans or the identities of their cohorts. Sometimes tiny, pin-sized dirks (*fukumi-bari*) were kept in the ninja's mouth the way carpenters hold tenpenny nails in their mouths, then spat or blown out at the eyes of the enemy. Other dirks, about the size of a ballpoint pen, were held inside the hand along the palm and thrown with a smooth, stiff-arm motion.

Female ninja used long, deadly looking hairpins to assassinate their victims, much as the Finnish double-agent heroine in Len Deighton's "Billion Dollar Brain" did away with her victims. The latter's trick was to go to bed with her target for the night, trickle her left hand down his spine until she found the vulnerable spot, then slyly remove her hairpin with her right hand and plunge it into the spot in the spine where the fingers of her left hand were touching. Kunoichi, of course, didn't limit their target to the spine, but included the heart, eyes, ears, temples, etc. Both sexes also used metal claws which fit over the ends of their fingers and were held in place with animal skin backing. Some ninja, however, let their natural finger nails and toenails grow long and kept them filed to a sharp point.

One of the most original ninja weapons was the poison water gun. Designed to blind the eyes of the enemy, it was a bamboo tube about a foot-and-a-half long, open at one end and closed at the business end except for a small hole in the center. The ninja poured the poison water which he concocted himself into the tube. Then taking a length of bamboo with a smaller diameter and with a piece of rag fitted onto the front end, he inserted it a few inches into the rear, and open, end. When the enemy came within range, about 60 feet, the ninja shoved home the inserted piece, forcing the poison water out through the small hole in a jet spray and blinding the enemy before the latter had time to realize what was happening and duck out of the way. The poison water ammunition consisted of iron powder and a liquid mixture used for staining the teeth of married women.

CRUDE GUNS of wood which fired iron balls, below left, were sometimes light enough to be held in a man's arms and fired like a bazooka. Like the American Indians, ninja used fire arrows, below right, to start fires, such as the one at the top of the photo. The explosive arrow, at center, was fired into the ranks of the enemy to frighten the troops and their horses. Another kind of explosive arrow is on the bottom. Leaves acted as a sort of propeller with powder at the tip.

LIGHTLY-ARMED ninja (such as Yoshiaki Hatsumi, in this case, with the short sword) were often cornered by confident swordsmen who raised their big, two-handed weapons over their heads and smiled before the final, swift stroke. The doomed ninja, seconds away from death, would suddenly reach into their jackets and let loose a spray of powder to temporarily blind their antagonists. By the time the sputtering, cursing swordsmen could open their eyes again, the ninja had vanished—in a puff of smoke.

The ninja was not only skilled at using guns and explosives, but was also adept at devising his own explosive weapons. He developed smoke grenades, mines, explosive arrows, flashing balls and even firecrackers to confuse his opponents while escaping. But until gunpowder and firelocks were introduced by Portuguese traders in the mid-16th Century, the ninja was pretty much limited in the use of fire and smoke except as signal fires and torches as well as for incendiarism. But they did invent a sort of gun made from bamboo which had a range of less than 100 feet. After the Portuguese arrived, however, the ninja also used derringers and other hand guns.

Ninja firearms included bronze pistols (*futokoro-teppo*), which he carried in the breast of his uniform. Wooden guns were made from the hollowed-out trunks of trees, the barrel of which was bored and hooped with iron on the outside. Called *kozutsu,* the gun had a metal trigger and fired iron balls. Although some lighter versions could be held in a man's arms and fired like a bazooka, these wooden guns were generally too primitive to be very effective. Some stories tell of wooden cannons large enough to shoot a ninja through the air like the human cannonballs of the circus, but such tales are undoubtedly more fanciful than factual.

Surprisingly enough, ninja even used land mines. Called *jirai,* they contained a fused explosive charge in a strong wooden case with a thin top so that when placed underground it would explode upward. A firecracker, *torinoko,* shaped like an egg with a fuse attached, was used primarily to surprise the enemy with its loud bang. The *hyakurai-ju* was another unique weapon consisting of several small guns set in a circle inside a large wooden gun barrel. Fired by a fuse, it sounded like a string of Chinese firecrackers exploding, only louder. Indeed, the main idea was to make a lot of noise in order to startle the enemy and create as much panic and confusion as possible.

Ninja practitioner Nawa tells of how some ninja designed pistols with a knife blade attached below the barrel and extending out beyond it like a miniature bayonet. If the shot missed or only winged his adversary, the ninja could leap on him with the knife-end of the pistol.

Ninjitsu scholar Heishichiro Okuse divides the ninja's use of fire and explosives into six main categories: signal fires, torches, smoke bombs, flash bombs, sound bombs and incendiary bombs. But he also notes that they used rocket signals as well. A ninja had many kinds of torches at his disposal. The *mizu-taimatsu* was designed to burn even during rain, while a small, hand-palm torch (*tanagokoro-tai matsu*) was made so that the flame could easily be concealed by a ninja's hand, making it quite useful for close inspection at night. Ninja candles, *ninshokudai,* were shaped like the letter "L" so they could easily be hooked on a wall projection or on a tree in the garden.

Arrows were a favorite weapon of the ninja, and he used all kinds, including explosive, flaming and poison-tipped ones. Their bamboo bows were small and light so that they were easy to carry without losing their effectiveness. Much as the American Indians shot flaming arrows into forts and log cabins, the ninja also had fire arrows. He used them not only to start fires, but mixed them with explosive arrows for shooting into the ranks of the enemy to frighten the troops and their horses. Nawa claims ninja had a magazine system of firing four arrows at a time as well as a sort of rocket system based on a bamboo tube affixed to the arrow with an explosive charge. It was mostly used for signalling, rather than as a weapon.

Blinders thrown into the enemy's eyes by ninja included everything from pepper, sand and ashes to special powders concocted by the ninja himself. The blinders were usually kept in an egg-shaped container and carried in a breast pocket for quick and easy access in time of need. Many a swordsman has cornered an apparently unarmed ninja, then raised his big, two-handed sword over his head and smiled confidently before the final, swift downward stroke. The doomed ninja, seconds away from death, suddenly reaches inside his jacket and out flashes a small, egg-shaped container. And before his enemy can bring down the sword, the ninja lets loose a spray of powder that blinds his antagonist. By the time the sputtering, cursing swordsman can open his eyes again, the ninja has vanished – in a puff of smoke.

Web of Subterfuge

The ninja had a staggering variety of special devices useful to him in his work. He had all sorts of grappling hooks and ropes for scaling walls and gaining entrance to castles. Some of the more remarkable devices he used were those for crossing water. So adept was the ninja at crossing moats, rivers and lakes that legend had it he could actually walk on water.

But like all the tales and legends according the ninja supernatural powers – flying, living underwater like a fish, vanishing in a puff of smoke, sinking into the ground, flowing through stone walls and transforming himself into a snake, frog, bird or insect – the claim that he could walk on water also had a basis of truth in it. Indeed, there are logical explanations for all of these supposedly super-human feats.

Actually, the ninja had a number of water-crossing devices. One was the *ukidaru* or, simply, floating pots. He would encase his feet in waterproof reed pots tightly woven for the purpose and then use a fan-like oar made of bamboo to help him "walk" across the moat. Another water-crossing device was a contraption resembling a life jacket. Usually

EXAGGERATED STORIES claiming ninja could walk on water might have stemmed from their use of the ukidaru, or floating pots, to cross swamps and marshlands, as above, or even castle moats. The center of the water spider, or mizugumo, at right, was strapped onto the ninja's feet.

70

WATER-CROSSING DEVICES included air-filled skins, floating pots, wooden water spiders for the feet and rafts. At right a ninja vigorously applies his versatile bamboo fan-oar to row himself across a small lake in a contraption resembling a life jacket.

BAMBOO TUBES were used to breathe through while swimming underwater "like a fish". Ninja also used Japanese-style reeds, tobacco pipes and even their sword scabbards which had removable tips.

made of rabbit or horse skins and filled with air, it was divided into four parts. One section was strapped on each side of the ninja and a third at his rear. He straddled the fourth section and went to work with his trusty bamboo oar. These feudal-age "water-wings" came in handy, especially when crossing an enemy castle's moat at night.

Water Spiders

Another unique device for crossing water was called *mizugumo,* or water spider. It consisted of four curved sections of wood fastened together to form a circle with a hole at the center. A rectangular piece of wood as long as a man's foot was affixed in the center and held with pieces of cord. The ninja then strapped his feet on the rectangular center piece and proceeded to walk across the water.

Present-day ninja scholar Heishichiro Okuse doubts its effectiveness, however, claiming that the water spiders would be unable to support the weight of a man. Needless to say, if these wooden floats were forced below the surface of the water, it would be virtually impossible for the ninja to keep his balance let alone lift his foot up to take a step forward.

Other contraptions included small, one-man rafts (*kameikada*) made by crossed bamboo or timber sections and floated by four large ceramic jars sealed so as to be watertight. But this device had several drawbacks. It was large, bulky and easily spotted; therefore, it could only be used at night. It was heavy, too, making it difficult to carry any great distance. The ninja also had a collapsible craft called *kyobako-fune.* It resembled a wooden chest made waterproof by its fur covering. Since it was fairly light and easily transported, it probably found much more use than the one-man raft.

There has always been some interest in how well people hundreds of years ago could swim. Although it has been claimed that the ancient Assyrians used a stroke resembling the overhead crawl stroke, most swimmers from around the world have relied on the breaststroke or sidestroke style until just recently. The ninja were said to be accomplished swimmers, but kept themselves from being completely immersed as much as possible in order to prevent water damage to any powders and food they might be carrying. But when they did swim, they generally fitted the web-like *mizukaki* onto their feet, much as modern swimmers wear flippers, for speed swimming underwater as well as on the surface of the water. Some stories also claim ninja wore goggles and swam underwater like feudal-age frogmen, breathing from air-filled skins.

Ninja may also have used something on the order of the wooden floats a 70-year-old farmer wore a few years ago to cross a four-mile-wide strait separating Kobe from Awaji Island in the Seto Inland Sea. It took him four-and-a-half hours to cross Akashi Strait in the six-foot-long floats, so devised so that up-and-down movements of his feet propelled small paddles in the stern and sent him forward. He also had a rudder set up between the floats which he controlled with his right hand, while his left hand gripped a bamboo pole attached to the front of the floats for balance. The holes where his feet entered the floats were carefully sealed so no water could leak through.

Hooks and Ladders

The ninja had several climbing devices available, but two of the most common were ladders and ropes with hooks. There were many types of ladders, varying according to the purpose for which they were used. Rope ladders, of course, were the lightest and most easily managed, but ninja also used bamboo and wooden ladders as well as combinations of rope and bamboo or wooden ladders. All the ladders, except those made entirely of bamboo or wood, were collapsible.

The crosspieces on bamboo ladders were usually secured with cord. Rope ladders with wooden crosspieces were equipped with metal rings through which the wooden sections were inserted, then tied. But sometimes the rope was simply twisted open and the wooden crosspiece stuck through the loops on each side, with a knot tied above and below to prevent the wooden section from slipping down. These ladders sometimes had metal spikes at each crosspiece so they could be

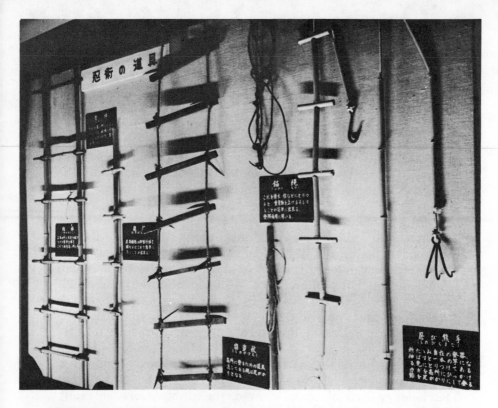

WALL-CLIMBING DEVICES such as the grappling hook, above right, could be turned into wicked weapons of personal defense. Ladders, at left, were made with combinations of wood, bamboo and rope. Various hooks and rakes, below left, were used by ninja to scale walls. At right is a tree-climbing device known as an ippon-sugi nobori.

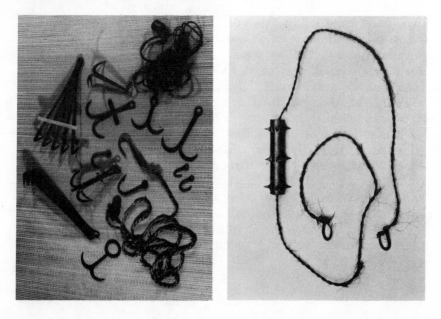

A "HUMAN FLY" was the attribute given the ninja who was adept at climbing walls, such as this one who scales the Hakuho Castle in Iga-Ueno. Ninja tied metal spikes, below left, around their tabi to aid in their climb. The ninja below right also wears tekagi, hooks, on his hands.

driven into the castle wall or cliff to prevent them from swaying from side to side.

Another type of ladder was a collapsible bamboo ladder with a rope running through the separate bamboo sections. Small bamboo crosspieces were fitted between the bamboo sections, with holes in the center of these crosspieces so that the rope would pass through them, too, and thus hold them in place.

The larger, more conventional ladders were generally used for descending from high places rather than for climbing, except when ninja worked in teams. The first man would climb the wall by rope, then pull up the ladder and tie it in place. In this way, the ladder could also be used for descending the other side of the castle wall. And when the ninja were making their escape, they would climb back up the inside of the wall, pull the ladder up and let it down the outside of the wall. The last ninja would drop the ladder and climb down by rope which could then be snapped up and down or from side to side until the hook freed itself.

When working alone, the ninja usually carried only a rope with a metal grappling hook at one end. Sometimes knots would be tied at intervals in the rope to facilitate climbing walls, trees and the like. Hooks had a ring at the lower end through which the rope was tied.

Three types of hooks were commonly used: single hooks, double hooks and three-pronged hooks. The latter type sometimes had all three hooks pointed in the same direction like three iron talons of a claw, but in other versions each of the three hooks extended in a different direction so that no matter how it was thrown one of the three hooks would take hold.

The *kumade,* or rake, also served the same function as a hook. It was usually made so that four or five long metal pieces with hooks on the ends extended from a metal ring at the base. The rake was attached to a rope or separated sections of bamboo with a rope passing through and connecting them. Ropes were often made with braided women's hair for extra strength.

Rakes and hooks could also be turned into weapons in time of need when nothing else was at hand. An iron rake could easily tear a man's face to shreds or even disembowel him. One of the most effective dual-purpose ladder weapons was an oak staff seven or eight feet high with small metal crosspieces for steps and a large, vicious-looking hook attached to the top.

Swords with large, sturdy guards and slightly dull edges were often used in climbing. The ninja could either lay the sword against a small obstacle and step up on the guard in order to reach the top of the wall, or he could reverse the sword and use the guard as a hook and pull himself upward.

Sea-Escapes

The superstition that ninja could assume the powers of fish and live underwater has a perfectly logical explanation. For one thing, the ninja breathed through hollow reeds, bamboo shoots, sword scabbards and even long, narrow smoking pipes to stay underwater for long periods. When swimming underwater and such tubes were impractical for breathing through, the ninja might carry a skin inflated with air from which he would take breaths, much as a modern agent might use an aqualung.

The ninja often carried smoke bombs or packets of powder which he would throw at the enemy. They would explode in a cloud of smoke, temporarily blinding the enemy, and thus the ninja could "disappear in a puff of smoke" like a magician.

Legend has the ninja "flying like a bird", although a logical explanation can be made for this "feat". The ninja used his cape as a sort of parachute to carry him down great drops. He is also thought to have employed some sort of a sail device, or possibly even a man-sized kite, for soaring through the air. In something of the same vein, the ninja was often given the attributes of a "human fly", able to walk up the sides of walls and across ceilings. This, too, can be explained in sensible terms. He employed a number of special devices to aid him in breaking into houses, forts and castles. He wore soft, split-toed tabi which helped him find grips easily in climbing walls and cliffs.

One of the most famous Ninjitsu devices was the *tekagi*, or *shuko,* a metal band which slipped around one or both hands, with metal spikes protruding from the palm side. The spikes could be used for getting a grip on the side of a wall or for gripping a beam in the ceiling and moving hand-over-hand across a room without touching the floor. It could also be used for climbing high trees. Spikes tied to the bottom of the tabi or sandals were sometimes used in conjunction with tekagi so that both the ninja's hands and feet could dig into the wall, ceiling or tree.

As mentioned in the previous chapter, tekagi could also be turned into a wicked weapon in a hand-to-hand encounter. A sword or knife thrust could be parried by the metal band around one hand, while the other spiked hand could rake the enemy's face.

Ninja also stretched a rope equipped with a large pulley and handgrip across chasms or from a tree to the top of a castle wall. Since one end of the rope was secured higher than the other, he could zip across by hanging onto the pulley. It was used as part of an escape route or when a team of ninja had to cross an obstacle such as a gulley, moat, river, etc. This device, too, could have been behind stories of flying ninja.

The ninja also employed other special devices such as a sort of skeleton key for unlocking warehouse doors, various kinds of saws, a chisel and a spade-like, digging device known as a *kunashi*. Ropes were not only used for climbing but also for securing doors from the outside as well as for tying up captured enemies. The Ninja knew hundreds of different knots and tying methods as well as how to escape from them by dislocating his joints.

Smoke Signals

In communicating with each other ninja not only made smoke signals by day from hilltops and bonfires at night but also sent up rocket signals as well. Of course, conventional means were used, too; couriers on horseback, on foot or by boat, messenger pigeons, etc.

The most familiar trademark of the ninja was the black costume he wore. The jacket, somewhat resembling the modern judo jacket, was equipped with various pockets for

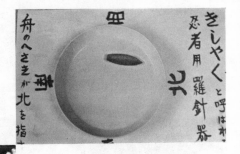

きしやくと呼は
忍者用 羅針器
舟のへさえが北を指す

READY FOR ACTION, a ninja is protected with an undergarment of chain mail since he was often called on to fight in regular battlefield combat. Above is a kishiyaku, a kind of ninja compass marked by the four directions. Other typical devices carried by the ninja were his sword, at bottom; tetsu-bishi (caltrops), at right; shuriken and a pouch, at center; a rope with a grappling hook, at lower left; and a rope-and-bamboo climbing device, upper left.

PROTECTED, even on the back of his hands, this ninja prepares to engage in unarmed combat. The typical combat costume, below, included large, chain mail gloves, leggings and jacket.

holding a wide variety of weapons and devices such as shuriken, blinding powder, food, medicine, etc. A black hood covered the face with a pair of slits for the eyes. A black hakama skirt worn like trousers and leggings covered the lower part of the body, while the feet were concealed in black tabi and sandals.

Altogether, the ninja had six main pieces of clothing: the mask, a body protector, *hakama* (a divided skirt for formal wear by men), protectors, belt and tabi. The clothing as well as all attachments carried were black. Even the sandals he wore were black and cushioned with cotton padding so the ninja could walk as silently as possible. A pliable armor of chain mail was worn as underwear.

Besides using special pockets for carrying needed weapons and supplies, the ninja also brought along a bag. Inside were a rope with a hook, slate pencil, drugs, *tetsubishi* (caltrops), shuriken, spare hooks, nails, metal weights, blinding powder and a digging tool. He wore his sword on his belt or slung across his back. In wintertime he carried a *doka* – a pocket heater consisting of an outer shell of iron and burning coals inside. It was used to keep his hands warm and also to set off explosives. In addition, he carried a three-foot-long towel and canteen of Japanese green tea.

Since the ninja was often called upon to fight alongside the soldier on the battlefield, he was also equipped with a combat uniform. He wore a jacket and leggings of chain mail. His wrists, hands and neck were also protected by mail guards, and his headpiece was made of mail as well. A unique touch was the metal chin guard. All in all, his combat costume was a formidable outfit.

In winter when snow covered the ground, the ninja clothed himself entirely in white, like the mountain ski troops of Finland. This snow uniform differed from his regular outfit only in color and footwear. The ninja wore snowshoes that consisted of white tabi on which were tied metal blades for easy walking on hard snow or ice. Instead of leaving a footprint in the snow, they left only a puzzling series of five parallel marks. Normally, for walking on ice, ninja tied on a double-bladed device, one at the front and one at the back of the foot, to enable him to keep his balance more easily.

Thus, the ninja was a clever chameleon prepared to attack at any season and equipped with a bagfull of special devices as well as a wide assortment of weapons. But, more often than not, it was his brilliant strategems and tactics that helped him escape from the most dangerous predicaments and gain him final success.

Poisons
and Curatives

Every ninja was an accomplished pharmacist, skilled in preparing different poisons and special powders and compounds. His training in *yagen* (pharmacy) also allowed him to prepare gunpowder and explosives, medicines and even concentrated, dehydrated foods for use on long missions.

Poisons were made from mineral, plant and animal sources. They were potent enough to kill, but could be weakened so that they only put the enemy to sleep, paralyzed him or made him shake with laughter. Dirks, darts and arrows were tipped with poison for assassinations. Poisons were mixed with food and drink, and even poisoned flowers were used. Curatives and medicines were concocted from herbs and *shochu* (unrefined sake), among other things.

One of the strangest poisons was based on Japanese green tea. Called *gyokuro,* its recipe sounds like something from an old wives' tale. The brewed green tea was put in a canteen and buried for 30 to 40 days, then mixed in *miso-shiru* (soybean paste used in making miso soup), Japanese tea or water and given to the victim. Usually designed for sick people, it quickly took effect on them after it was drunk.

Although it was potent enough to kill them in a couple of days, it could even make a healthy man take sick after a month or so and eventually die in about 70 days.

A more effective poison called *zagarashi-yaku* made use of a green plum or peach. It was made both as a solid as well as a powder and was mixed with food. Since it had an immediate fatal effect, it was often used at banquets to kill off many persons at the same time.

Other poisonous ingredients used by the scheming ninja, according to Okuse, included the green rust (patina) from copper, arsenic, lycorie radiate (a type of autumn flower), buttercup and wolfbane. Swords, spears and daggers were sometimes tipped with horse dung and blood, just as the Viet Cong even today use excrement to tip their bamboo spikes in jungle foot and body traps. A person cut by a blade dipped in horse dung and blood developed an infection almost immediately, leading to lockjaw and, finally, death.

Witches' Brew

The ninja were probably the first inventors of poison gas, although it was used more as an anaesthetic to put victims to sleep than to kill them. Although this one sounds like something concocted by the three witches in *Macbeth,* it was apparently effective. The blood of a newt, mole and snake were mixed, then absorbed by paper. When the paper was set on fire, it gave off fumes guaranteed to put the enemy to sleep. Ninja used it in bedrooms for putting the victim into a deep sleep. The ninja also tossed some of the magic paper into a stove of glowing charcoal in the guardhouse to make the guards drowsy and fall asleep.

Even more weird was the following recipe for sending ninja victims off to the land of nod:
- the powder of three male rats
- several leaves of the paulownia tree
- one fat centipede
- a handful of cotton seeds
- several scoops of yellow cattle dung

This poisonous mess was compressed into a ball and dried, and when the powder scraped off this ball was burnt, anyone inhaling the fumes slipped off to sleep.

Liquid sleep potions were also devised by the busy ninja. One involved taking hemp leaves, drying them in the shade and then grinding them into a powder. A liquid was made from the powder and mixed with light Japanese green tea.

Something of the effect of these sleeping and numbing potions can be understood from Shakespeare's description of one that Friar Lawrence gives to Juliet:

"And this distilled liquor drink thou off;
When presently through all thy veins shall run
   a cold and drowsy humour, for no pulse shall
   keep his native progress, but surcease;
No warmth, no breath shall testify thou liv'st;
The roses in thy lips and cheeks shall fade to
   paly ashes; thy eyes' windows fall,
Like death, when he shuts up the day of life;
Each part, depriv'd of supple government,
Shall stiff and stark and cold, appear like death;
And in this borrow'd likeness of shrunk death
Thou shalt continue two-and-forty hours,
And then awake as from a pleasant sleep."

Thus, it can readily be assumed that similar potions to put a man to sleep were well known in Europe, virtually contemporaneous with their use by Japanese ninja, for the Bard's lifetime parallels the final golden and twilight years of the ninja, from 1564 to 1616.

Some of the ingredients of poisons used by ninja to numb their victims or bring on temporary paralysis include the body fluid from the projection over the eyes of a toad and the liquid from the guts of a blowfish, or globe-fish. The potency of the blowfish liquid as a poison can be attested to by the fact that more than 100 persons die in Japan every year from eating raw blowfish *(sashimi)*. If the fish has not been properly cleaned, the poisonous liquid penetrates the flesh which is then eaten by the unsuspecting gourmet. Blowfish restaurants are strictly regulated by the government and accidents occur only when amateurs try to clean the fish.

The ninja never missed a trick, even being prepared

SKILLED in the art of yagen (pharmacy), the ninja was trained to concoct his own poisons and curative medicines, as demonstrated by Yoshiaki Hatsumi, at right. On long missions the ninja carried protein-rich energy food such as tofu (a soft soybean curd), which Hatsumi is eating and also shown below left, and genmai juice, below in the small bamboo container.

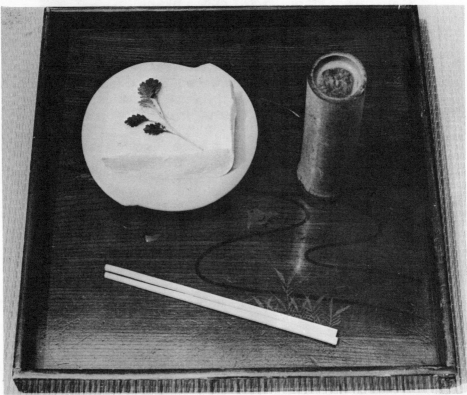

at times to harass his enemy with itching poisons. This was usually nettle-thorn powder and was scattered on his neck. Although it wasn't fatal, it still caused a maddening itch down the back of the victim. Laughing gas used to be a popular anaesthesia with dentists a few decades ago, but the ninja had brewed a mixture that produced the same effect hundreds of years before. They took what is called a "laughing mushroom," shredded it and mixed it with the food. When the enemy took a few bites of it, he erupted into a laughing fit that left him weak and helpless to resist whatever else might follow.

One of the most terrifying poisons was designed to drive the victim mad, but since there is still danger that the recipe might fall into the wrong hands, it remains a closely-guarded secret. Even today, only a handful of men, including Okuse, know how it was made. At any rate, five to ten seeds of an unspecified plant were taken, ground into a powder and mixed with food. A few hours after it had been consumed, the enemy slowly but surely became temporarily insane.

There are many plants today that are commonly recognized as poisonous. These include poison ivy and poison oak, hemlock, poison sumac, belladonna, henbane, strychnos, etc.

The best way for a ninja to stay alive was to remain anonymous, to disguise himself when he ventured abroad during the day and make himself as elusive as possible on night missions. It therefore stands to reason that he couldn't drag himself to the nearest doctor whenever he was wounded or sick for fear of being identified and thus compromising his mission.

Of necessity, then, the ninja learned how to doctor his own wounds and devise his own remedies and cures. For sword wounds he mixed an herb root called goosefoot with a plant named black cowpea in equal quantities, charred it and then painted it on the wound. Or he might spread mashed narcissus roots on the sword wound.

Bamboo cuts were treated by pasting wheat flour mixed with water on the wound, especially to relieve the pain. Mashed leeks were used on gunshot wounds. To stop the flow of blood from nail cuts and scratches the ninja used the smoke from slow-burning rags. To relieve the pain from scaldings he painted a mixture of tannin and India ink on the wound. A more complex remedy for stopping the flow of blood was to mix the powder of dried paulownia leaves with the leaves of the Japanese tea plant mashed by the teeth. This was then put on the bleeding wound.

Since a ninja's life was full of danger, it is not surprising that he was occasionally wounded by enemy swords, spears, arrows, knives, staves, etc. At the same time, he was sometimes injured accidentally by making a hurried escape. He might fall while trying to scale a wall, slip against a jagged rock in attempting to elude pursuers, scratch his face on thorns or cut an arm on a sharp branch, and so on.

A plant called fhellodindron amurense was used for sprains and contusions. Half of the quantity to be used was mashed and the other half left in its raw state. Both were mixed with vinegar and painted on the sprain or contusion. If a wound became infected and there was danger of lockjaw developing, the cure was to take the skin of a loach (mudfish) and paste it on the infected part, changing to a new piece of skin often. This was also effective in treating Rose's disease.

Fighting Fire With Fire

In cases of food poisoning the remedy was amazingly simple. If the ninja suffered from bonito poisoning, for instance, he would eat charred bonito. If he were poisoned by eating boar, then he ate charred boar. This principle is used by modern medicine today in treating such ailments as snake bite with an antidote made of poison from the same snake. And vaccines are usually made up of the same virus which they are trying to prevent.

The ninja even had a remedy for cancer. A piece of an old trunk of wisteria, especially a lump growing on the trunk, was ground into a powder, then mixed with water and drunk. Other cancer cures consisted of taking five grains of waternut seed powder every day with water. The seeds of water chestnuts, or water caltrops, were sometimes substituted for waternut seeds. Here, again, the lump on the wisteria trunk is a kind of plant cancer so that the same principle of using fire to fight fire was applied in this case, too.

When a ninja went out on a long mission, he had to take along emergency rations, a sort of feudal-age K-rations. On a 10-day trip, for example, he might pack his pouch with the following energy foods: 30 parts of bleached rice, 5 parts of wheat flour, 30 parts of dried bonito, 30 parts of dried trout, 30 parts of dried plum and 30 parts of powder made from the tender part of pine.

Other protein-rich foods the ninja subsisted on included *tofu,* a soft curd made of soybeans and still a popular part of the Japanese diet today. A small bamboo section might be used to carry *genmai juice* made of unpolished rice. Another energy-producing food was *tsune no mizu* made from *umeboshi,* or Japanese plum. It was carried in raw bamboo which produced a sort of vitamin-creating chemical reaction.

Typical thirst quenchers on the ninja's list were peppermint powder, arrowroot starch and salted plum, all mixed together into a powder and made into a ball. Three grains a day were expected to quench the ninja's thirst when a ready supply of water was not available. Another trick was to bite a leek and paint the juice in the nostrils. Thirty sesame seeds were also supposed to temporarily relieve thirst.

Blinding powders for throwing into an enemy's eyes included ordinary pepper, sand and ashes as well as poisons from minerals, animals, insects and plants. The liquid poison used in ninja water guns consisted of iron powder and a mixture used to stain black the teeth of married women.

Fortunately, some of the recipes have survived for many of the medicines, curatives and energy foods and undoubtedly are still used in some parts of Japan. This is especially so since the popularity of herb and folk medicines, including Chinese medicine, has recently been revived.

Physical and Mental Training

The young ninja apprentice started training by the time he was barely able to walk. He learned to dislocate his joints in order to slip out of his bonds in case he was captured on a mission. At the same time, he was taught to use all the ninja weapons and special devices, climb trees, swim, ride horses, wrestle and fight without weapons, remain submerged underwater for extended periods, cover long distances without tiring, scale walls and cliffs, and so on. He was also schooled in making drugs, medicines, poisons, explosives, blinding powders and energy foods, and also how to disguise himself.

His was a rugged, Spartan existence, being put through the paces in preparation for the rigors of a ninja life. He learned how to endure the cold, to fast without complaint, to hide for long periods without moving, to breathe imperceptibly, to make use of anything at hand in escaping and to steel himself against confessing under torture. In short, the youthful ninja developed the ability to survive by becoming a perfectionist in everything connected with his existence – a super-athlete, a flawless fighting machine and an intelligent, quick-thinking secret agent.

AN ALL-AROUND BUDO-
MAN, the ninja was an experi-
enced marksman in kyujitsu,
the art of archery. Bows were
small, light and portable, but
the arrows were deadly, sometimes being tipped with poison.
Below are the geta, or wooden
clogs, which ninja wore on ice
to attain perfect waist balance
and silent treading.

UNARMED COMBAT techniques are taught by Yoshiaki Hatsumi as part of his Togakure-ryu style of Ninjitsu. Above, Hatsumi comes to close quarters with his attacker and grasps him on the left shoulder. Suddenly, he jumps up onto his opponent and straddles him with both legs, immediately applying a strong scissors to try to crush a few ribs. Hatsumi then releases his grip and falls over backward, both legs still locked in the scissors grip. After releasing the scissors, he uses his legs to push his enemy over onto his back. At the same time, he slams the heel of his left foot into his rival's chin or face.

NINJA

The ninja of olden times, according to Yoshiaki Hatsumi, one of Japan's few remaining ninja practitioners, was the perfect, all-around athlete of his day, an expert in running, jumping, swimming, climbing walls, hiking long distances, throwing, etc. The 1964 Japanese Olympic team was so impressed by ninja training methods it seriously considered using several of them.

Perforce the ninja excelled in every one of the martial arts of his day: *kenjitsu* (swordsmanship), *iaijitsu* (fast-sword draw), *kyujitsu* (archery), *yarijitsu* (spear fighting), *bisento* (fighting with wide-bladed spear), *bojitsu* (stick fighting) and *kusari-gama* (skill with chain and scythe). At the same time, he was skilled in hand-to-hand combat, using wrestling and boxing techniques that were the forerunners of jujitsu, judo and karate.

During the rise of the shogun and the bushi in the 13th Century, sumo wrestling was converted into a rough, offensive martial art from which some say jujitsu and eventually judo developed. A close inspection will show that many of the judo throws today closely resemble those of its sumo progenitor. In the Kamakura Period (1192-1333) and subsequent eras, samurai warriors learned sumo techniques for practical, unarmed combat on the battlefield. Thus, the newly developed martial art, called *kumi-uchi*, was simply a means of boosting the samurai's fighting efficiency.

The Family Tree

Ninjitsu was handed down from father to son as a secret martial art. Several ninja clans arose, led by the great Iga and Koga clans, and it goes without saying that the various secrets of these ninja family groups were closely guarded. The ninja of one clan would often be in the hire of a local lord and thus pitted against the ninja of a rival clan in the employ of an enemy lord. Each clan tended to specialize in its own techniques since it always paid at such times to have a few secrets in one's bag of tricks that were not generally known to other ninja.

Ninja went through rigid training sessions to learn their techniques, usually at secret camps set up deep in the

DEFENSE AGAINST
A FRONT CHOKE

1. Yoshiaki Hatsumi is attacked by an enemy who grabs him around the neck and tries to choke him.

2. Countering the choke, Hatsumi simultaneously slaps both of his rival's ears, a very dangerous blow to apply since it can break the opponent's eardrums.

3. When the slap fails to break the enemy's grip, Hatsumi grabs the back of his antagonist's head and smashes his forehead into his rival's face.

4. Although the enemy is felled, Hatsumi keeps on the alert and is poised to strike another blow if the need arises.

DEFENSE FROM A PRONE POSITION

1. In a maneuver similar to judo's tomoe-nage, Hatsumi crouches low and braces himself as he grasps his enemy's midsection with both hands. He then falls backward to a point where his opponent is poised directly overhead.

2. Following through with the throw, Hatsumi pulls the enemy hard onto his head, knocking him senseless.

DEFENSE AGAINST
A KICK

1. An attempted kick by the enemy is blocked by Hatsumi's counter-kick.

2. Hatsumi retaliates further with a yubi, or thumb blow, to the opponent's exposed right side, just above the kidneys.

DEFENSE AGAINST
A REAR CHOKE

1. The enemy attacks from the rear with a strangle hold.

2. Quickly spreading his legs, Hatsumi snaps his right leg across his enemy's right leg and braces himself. He then grabs his opponent's arm with both hands.

3. In a powerful throw, Hatsumi suddenly pulls his enemy over his right shoulder.

4. Hatsumi follows through with his counter by grabbing his rival's right arm and slamming his right heel into the enemy's ribs to put him out of action.

DEFENSE AGAINST
A HIP THROW

1. When the enemy attempts to pull Hatsumi over his right hip, the latter extends his right leg to block the throw.

2. Hatsumi then counters with a yubi blow to his enemy's exposed right kidney.

DEFENSE AGAINST
A FIST STRIKE

1. His right hand curled into a fist, Hatsumi prepares to defend himself against the enemy.

2. As his opponent strikes with his right, Hatsumi quickly blocks the blow with his left arm.

3. Hatsumi immediately counters with a powerful koppo chopping blow with his right, breaking his enemy's right arm.

4. As usual, Hatsumi is poised to strike another potent blow in case the enemy revives and tries to attack again.

mountains away from the prying eyes of enemy ninja. During its halcyon days from the 15th to 17th Centuries there were more than 25 different Ninjitsu schools scattered throughout central Japan, with most of them situated in Iga and Koga Provinces. Daily training at these schools was focused on becoming adept in the use of the sword, bow and arrow, spear and shuriken and other weapons. Close attention was also paid to wall-climbing and river-crossing techniques as well as the use of numerous special devices. They also learned to become expert horsemen, swimmers, pharmacists, etc.

Super-human Skills

The late Seiko Fujita, who claimed he was the 14th master of the Koga School of Ninjitsu, said ninja could walk the 350 miles between Edo (now Tokyo) and Osaka in three days. Granted that is stretching things a bit, but Hatsumi insists that ninja could easily cover 75 miles a day. This is not too incredible when one recalls that Alexander the Great's army was capable of making a forced march of 75 miles in one day. Fujita said they trained day and night to attain super-human skills. "If the Japanese athletes of the present age trained as hard as ninja," he said, "I'm sure they could win all the major Olympic events." To improve his speed and skill in walking, the ninja practiced by leaning his body forward or to one side so that he was forced to walk rapidly to maintain his balance.

Ninja also trained by walking with *geta* (wooden clogs) on ice to achieve perfect waist balance and silent treading. Their sandals were specially cushioned with cotton cloth so they could walk or jump noiselessly. When skirting a wall or the side of a building, they kept their backs pressed against the wall and moved sideways to prevent detection.

The ninja were also great second-story men. They were master burglars when it came to breaking into enemy castles, spending many long hours practicing wall-scaling techniques. They also stressed leaping in their training to develop the ability to jump across rooftops and to avoid their enemies by leaping across narrow chasms, over low walls and fences, etc. Wider chasms were spanned by ninja teams securing a

SEIZED by an enemy from behind, a ninja prepares his defense in a demonstration by two of Yoshiaki Hatsumi's students.

SNAPPING his right leg across the front of his adversary's right leg, the ninja twists loose from the head grip and grasps his enemy's right arm with both of his hands.

LOWERING his shoulders, the ninja pulls his antagonist to the ground in a quick throw resembling judo's seoi-nage.

MAGICAL IN-SIGNS made
with the fingers to assist the
ninja in self-control during
moments of danger were an
intricate part of kuji-kiri.
Toshitsuga Takamatsu knits
his fingers into one of these
special signs. Below, a booklet
issued by the Iga-Ueno ninja
museum illustrates nine of the
81 different knittings: sha, to,
hei, rin (from top left), zai,
retsu, jin, kai (from bottom left)
and zen at far right.

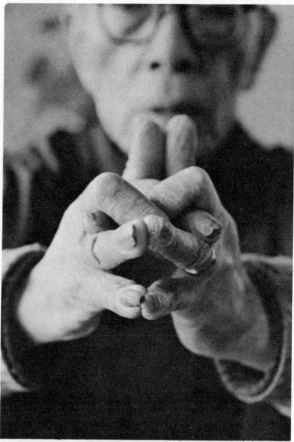

者　斗　兵　臨

前

在　列　陣　皆

rope on either side and then zipping across on a pulley. Fujita claimed that ninja became such experts at leaping many of them could jump over seven feet, which would make them champion high jumpers even today.

Ninja developed the technique of reduced breathing, enabling them to stay underwater for extended periods, up to five minutes, without having to breathe through reeds or take breaths from inflated skins. Pearl divers, who descend to considerable depths and are constantly active while underwater, have been known to hold their breath longer than three minutes. Thus, it is not inconceivable that a man lying motionless only a few feet underwater could hold out even longer without taking a breath.

Yoshiaki Hatsumi at his Ninjitsu dojo in Noda City, Chiba Prefecture, teaches unarmed combat in the Togakure-ryu style of Ninjitsu, one school of ancient ninja techniques. For instance, when faced with an adversary, the ninja comes to close quarters and grasps him on the left shoulder. Then he suddenly leaps up onto his opponent and straddles him with both legs, immediately applying a strong scissors grip to try to crush a few ribs. After relaxing his hold he falls over backward with both legs still locked in the scissors grip. On letting go, he uses his legs to push his enemy over onto his back. At the same time, he slams the heel of his left foot into his rival's chin or face.

"Battering Ram"

In another hand-to-hand combat technique the ninja defends himself with *Togakure-ryu* tactics. When his opponent tries to choke him by grabbing him by the collar, he counters by slapping both ears of his rival simultaneously – a very dangerous blow to apply since it can break the opponent's eardrums. If the slap misses, the ninja uses his hands to seize his opponent's head and pull it downward. The hardheaded ninja then uses his forehead as a battering ram to smash into his opponent's face.

If his enemy prepares to hit him with his right fist, the ninja quickly blocks the blow with his left arm, then counters with a powerful koppo chopping blow with his right hand, breaking his opponent's arm. And if his rival tries to kick him with his right foot, he blocks it with his own right counterkick. The ninja then attacks his enemy's ribs with a left, open-fisted blow.

One of Hatsumi's ninja techniques is reminiscent of the *tomoe-nage* of judo. The ninja crouches low and braces himself as he seizes his enemy's midsection with both hands. He then falls backward so that his enemy is poised directly overhead midway through the throw. Following through, the ninja pulls his enemy over hard onto his head, knocking him senseless. In another technique his enemy tries to pull him over the right hip, but the ninja spreads his legs so that his left leg blocks the throw. He then counters with a *yubi* technique, or sharp blow with the thumb, to his enemy's exposed right kidney.

If an enemy attacks from the rear, the ninja spreads his legs and braces himself, then grasps his attacker's arms. He counters by suddenly pulling his enemy over his right shoulder, as in judo's *seoi-nage,* following through by grabbing his rival's right arm and slamming his heel into his enemy's ribs to put him out of action.

Ninja put just as much, if not more, stress on the spiritual and mental aspects of Ninjitsu as they did on purely physical action. They had to have their wits about them at all times and work out complicated problems on the spot. They learned to sharpen their perception and psychological insight, developing their instincts to a point that seemed almost super-human.

One of the most interesting psychic and mystical aspects of Ninjitsu was *kuji-kiri*. These magical in-signs made with the fingers were used by ninja to hypnotize an adversary into inaction or temporary paralysis of action. There were some 81 different ways of knitting the fingers together. The ninja also uttered an incantation, often a Buddhist sutra, and drew alternately five horizontal and four vertical lines in the air with the fingers. *Kuji,* the number "nine", was said to be the most important number in *Shugendo* (mountain asceticism) and *Mikkyo* (esoteric Buddhism).

Also referred to as *jujitsu* (no connection to the martial art of the same name) kuji-kiri served to restore the ninja's confidence in himself and give him inner strength in moments of desperation and danger. It was even said to be capable of sharpening the ninja's perception and psychological insight so that he could sense hidden hostility, foresee the imminent death of a sick or aged person and even predict the breakup of a marriage.

The "Eyes of God"

Hatsumi claims kuji-kiri helped the ninja develop instincts similar to the sensitivity of primitive animals, and he was probably referring to this mystique of Ninjitsu when he said, "By learning Ninjitsu, one comes to know how to foresee the future. One finally gets the 'Eyes of God'." Jay Gluck, writer and critic in the Orient, notes that one of the arts developed by ninja was *sai-min jitsu*, a kind of hypnotic art.

Heishichiro Okuse, perhaps the foremost authority on Ninjitsu and author of four books on the subject, wrote his last ninja work on the theme "Hidden Ninjitsu – The Secret Thoughts and Strategies of the Ninja". According to him, ninja regarded nothing as impossible and scientifically applied brain power to every problem they encountered. Okuse regards these non-physical aspects of Ninjitsu as the key to a successful ninja career.

Strategy

It was his cunning and deception that was often to give the ninja the edge over his enemies, according to ninja scholar Okuse. These truths were emphasized and sharpened during the amazing training in espionage tactics that the ninja underwent. The ninja raised espionage to a highly-developed art centuries before such thorough training was given to cloak-and-dagger agents in Western countries.

Organized along strict military lines, ninja were divided into three ranks: *jonin,* leaders; *chunin,* subleaders; and *genin,* ordinary agents. The jonin maintained an extensive intelligence network, made contacts with the warlords to engage in spying and subversive activities, and then sent out his chunin and genin to fulfill these contracts.

It was an iron code of discipline that the ninja bound himself to. He was sworn to secrecy on the tactics of his art, and extreme steps were taken to ensure that the techniques did not pass into enemy hands. The fate for disloyalty was swift and certain. The informer was relentlessly tracked down and put to death.

Three essential qualifications were demanded of a ninja:

SPECIAL COMBAT TECHNIQUES and instructions are drawn on this ancient scroll, part of the secret documents handed down by ninja clans. Called tori-make, or make-mono, they belong to Yoshiaki Hatsumi, one of the handful of ninja practitioners left in Japan today.

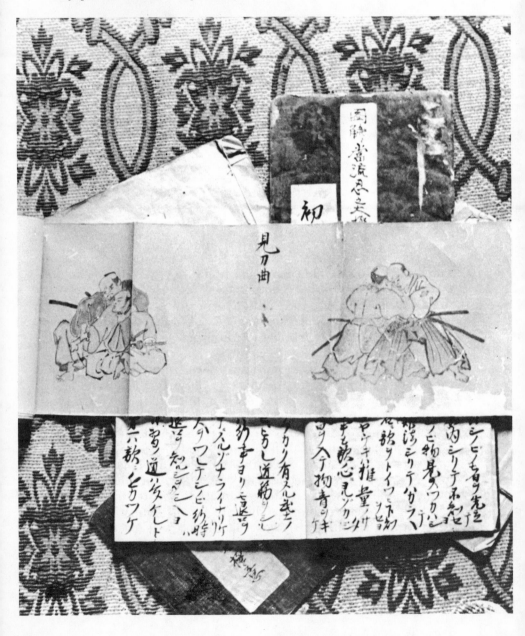

JAPANESE MATA HARIS played an important part in feudal times. This female ninja, or kunoichi, practices kuji-kiri.

a high sense of duty, a quick mind and a healthy, agile body able to undergo the rugged training demanded of a ninja. Nothing was considered too remote to be overlooked by the ninja if it could conceivably be used in helping him achieve his objective. Thoroughness was the key to ninja training, and special studies, tactics and strategies were developed to a point that would put to shame the training of modern-day secret agents.

Incredible as it sounds, the ninja was expected to develop the ability to predict the outcome of a struggle. Based on scientific premises, it involved the refinement of his insight into three key elements: earth, air and man. *Satten-jitsu,* or insight into the air, meant that the ninja understood how to take advantage of atmospheric conditions based on his knowledge of astrology, divination and meteorology.

The Koga school refers to the "foehn phenomenon" described by the dictionary as a warm, dry wind blowing down a mountain side. Well-known in the United States, this phenomenon is called a "santana" in the western part of the country. The ninja's ability to recognize this unique condition as conducive to the setting and rapid spread of fires enabled him to make use of it for setting the enemy camp ablaze. A dry season was also considered an ideal time for using fire to trap the enemy, drive him into an ambush or confuse and scatter his forces, then hunting them down piecemeal.

Windy nights were also propitious for incendiary work since fire spreads quickly and is difficult to contain, but the ninja first determined the direction of the wind so that a fire set on the edge of an encampment would spread inward or toward an area where most of the structures were located.

Yi (or I) Ching's **Book of Changes** (now translated into English) was available to the ninja. This book of Chinese divination, astrology and meteorology dealt with recognizing and taking advantage of atmospheric changes, among other things. Just as dry weather could be used to set fires, so, too, other types of weather could be put to good advantage by the ninja. Moonless nights, for example, were the best times for sneaking into an enemy castle or villa.

Clad in white and wearing sandals with metal blades tied on the bottom for easy walking, the ninja also ventured out during blizzards and snowy nights. Blending into the surrounding white landscape, he could easily slip past guards during such low-visibility conditions. Dark, stormy nights were also excellent for slipping into an enemy camp or launching a commando raid, especially if it rained since guards would be reluctant to stand out in the open and would cut their patrolling down to a minimum. All this the ninja was required to be aware of as part of *satten-jitsu.*

The Earth Principle

Observations and predictions founded on the earth principle were included in the ninja's *sacchi-jitsu* strategems. One of the most important points was the old military strategy of holding the high ground for a battle. Besides occupying high vantage points on land in preparation for an encounter, it also meant taking advantage of the natural features of the land, including ditches and rock formations, for hiding, escaping, ambushing, etc. Ninja, who often served as military consultants to warlords, naturally were expected to make themselves completely familiar with the terrain well before the impending battle or ambush.

Had a ninja been a consultant to the Duke of Wellington, for instance, he would have discovered the famous sunken road beforehand and devised a strategem to lure Napoleon's cavalry into it – deliberately. If he had been adviser to Gen. Robert E. Lee at Gettysburg he would have urged him to press his successful counterattack on the first day by dislodging the Union army from Cemetery Ridge before it could dig in and to immediately seize the strategic, flanking high ground of Culps Hill on one side and the Big and Little Round Tops on the other. And he certainly would have done his best to prevent Custer from riding into Sitting Bull's ambush at the Little Big Horn, for the ninja was not only adept at setting up an ambush, but was instinctively wary of stumbling into one.

Satsujin-jitsu, or insight into man, was more than just instant character analysis for the ninja. Since he was familiar with the science of physiognomy, he was able to read the facial features of his fellow-man. He dealt with people on a system of awards and punishments, dispensing one or the other

111

according to the personality and circumstances involved. He made it his business to know whether or not the enemy was strongly united, closely observing his character and sizing up his strengths and weaknesses, either as an individual or as a member of a group as well as the entire group itself.

Five Feelings

In dealing with people the ninja also operated on the *gojo-goyoku* principle of five feelings and five desires. The five feelings were actually character flaws and included targets who were likely to make costly mistakes or who were susceptible to bribery, blackmail, bullying and intimidation. They were people with a strong sensual appetite, a quick temper, a tender heart, a tendency toward laziness and a meek spirit.

The first of these, *kisha,* had to do with sensual pleasures and probably goes back to the first secret agent who ever tried to subvert a victim. Even today, it is one of the most popular methods of getting someone to spill his guts. Once the ninja learned that his enemy was a vain, self-indulgent person, he would do everything possible to cater to that weakness in his character. He flattered him, wined and dined him, and enticed him with beautiful women.

This was where the kunoichi, or female ninja agent, proved most useful. These Japanese Mata Hari were used for drawing secrets from the enemy or even for assassinating him. The beautiful ninja might be placed in the employ of the intended victim and there use all her feminine wiles to gain his good graces. Since it was the custom in those days for women to wear an elaborate hair-do similar to that worn by geisha today, it would be no problem for the kunoichi to conceal a long, sharp hairpin the size of a darning needle in her coiffure. After the enemy lord had satisfied himself and finally dropped off to sleep, the ever-watchful female ninja would take out the needle-like hairpin and stab him through the heart, eye, ear, temple or other mortal place. A male ninja might be sent into the castle or villa of the lord to help her escape or assist her in case something went wrong. It goes without saying that she had carefully "cased the joint" and worked out the best escape route well beforehand.

The *dosha* concept involved taking advantage of man's short temper, inducing him to something rash. Iago would have made a perfect ninja in the employ of a rival lord anxious to get jealous, hot-tempered Othello out of the way.

Using an overly sympathetic or soft-hearted person was termed *aisha*. Thus, a ninja might concoct some elaborate sob story in order to enlist the enemy's sympathy and thereby win his confidence.

A lazy enemy fond of idle amusements and entertainment was tempted with more of the same in what was known as *rakusha*. Hideyoshi Toyotomi, one of Japan's greatest samurai heroes, was in the process of uniting Japan in the late 16th Century, but had a lot of trouble taking Odawara Castle. Seeing that his long seige was getting nowhere fast, the clever general devised a strategem in which he held wild, all-night parties, full of lovely, laughing girls, out in the open and carefully within sight of his frustrated enemies who were manning the castle walls. The idea was to tempt the lazy, amusement-seeking soldiers among the enemy forces to desert or lose their fighting spirit. It came as no real surprise, then, when the Odawara Castle defenders capitulated a short time later.

Kyosha, or handling the cowardly, the meek and those unwilling to put their lives in jeopardy, was another kettle of fish. Ghengis Khan was probably the master of this strategem. The Mongolian leader, when sweeping through the cities of Persia and Arabia, gave each city a day or so to surrender. If they refused he would storm the walls and slaughter every living soul inside, then make a huge mound of their heads. The word soon got around so that after a while just his threats alone or his mere appearance on the horizon were enough to convince even the most stubborn city that it should open its gates to his Golden Horde.

Thus, dire threats would be aimed at the meek; sympathetic appeals to save the women and children at the soft-hearted; promises of a life of ease and idle entertainment at idlers; dares, challenges and insults at the short-tempered; and flattery and lures of fleshly pleasures at the vain and self-indulgent.

The five desires were centered around pride, wealth, sex,

pleasure and earthly appetite. As in the case with the five feelings, the ninja appealed to the fulfillment of these desires in order to use the victims to his own advantage.

Espionage

According to Okuse, there are six preparatory tactics used by the ninja in conducting espionage activities: anonymity, discovering enemy aims, collecting intelligence data, misleading the enemy, learning the enemy's favorite fighting tactics and preventing the tactics of his own lord from becoming predictable.

Mugei-mumei no jitsu means "no art - no name". One of the key secrets of success for the ninja was to remain anonymous which is the main reason so few ninja heroes enliven the pages of Japanese history. The ninja must not be recognized by friend or foe. Some were known to have slashed their faces on the point of being captured to prevent the enemy from identifying them. Others dislocated their jaws so they couldn't be forced to talk under torture. And when the ninja ventured out in public during the daylight hours, he invariably disguised himself. Thus, a ninja concealed his name, his technique and his objectives, even to the point of death. Two ninja from the same network might, each unaware that the other ninja was watching him, be assigned to the same mission with instructions to make sure that his friendly rival was not captured, even if he had to kill his confederate to prevent it from happening.

The ninja also made it his business to detect the aims and strategy of his enemy as soon as possible so that counter-measures could be taken in time to stop him from achieving his objective. Once a battle actually started, it might be too late.

Intelligence and counterintelligence activities were also important parts of the ninja's preparatory tactics. Ninja were sent out to collect as much data as possible and it was not unusual for the *jonin* (ninja leader) to dispatch two *genin* (ordinary agents) on separate missions to gather information about the enemy. In this case they would not be told about each other. The jonin then compared the data. This approach not only served to double-check the validity of the intelligence received, but also provided a more comprehensive, in-depth report. Vital information gaps were filled in this way that otherwise would have been overlooked if the job were handled by only one ninja. It also might uncover a ninja acting as a double-agent.

Another tactic cited by Okuse was to mislead the enemy as to the real objectives of the ninja's lord by providing false information. An important secret document might be "lost" so that the enemy would easily stumble on it, or a courier might deliberately allow himself to be captured while carrying battle plans from one ally to another. Sometimes, the ninja would disguise himself as an itinerant monk and pass on to an enemy officer information that he had picked up "while journeying through the allied camp". The information thus obtained by the enemy might contain the wrong date for the start of a battle, the wrong direction in which the allies planned to attack, an exaggeratedly low figure of allied strength or false plans for retreat. If the enemy seemed to swallow the bait, the allied side could then set up an ambush or launch a surprise attack.

In order that the allies might acquaint themselves with the enemy's tactics and style of maneuvering, the ninja would scout the enemy position and analyze his strength. He would also study the past tactics employed by the enemy as well as the kind of maneuvering he favored. On the basis of the ninja's report the allied side could then adjust its own strategy and tactics. For instance, if the enemy tended to separate his forces during a battle, the strategy would be to divide and conquer. If he kept his main battle line too thin, the allied side might try to smash through the center, or if the enemy concentrated most of his strength at the center, the allies would hit him on the flanks and roll up the battle line.

The sixth and last preparatory tactic employed by the ninja, according to Okuse, was to ensure that his own side did not standardize its tactics in order to prevent the enemy from becoming familiar with them. The allied general was urged to keep trying out new tactics or to modify his regular tactics enough to keep the enemy off-balance. By deliberately changing his favorite tactics from time to time the allied general could insure the unpredictability of his actions. Just when the enemy thought he had the allied tactics figured out, the allied general could trick the enemy into showing his hand, then suddenly trap him with an unexpected maneuver.

Hiding Behind God

One of the most clever strategems in the ninja's bag of tricks was called *kamigakure no jitsu*, or "hiding oneself behind God". In this case the ninja might be handed the dangerous assignment of assassinating an enemy lord. The lords in those bygone days were heavily guarded, both by samurai and their own ninja. As a result it might be far too risky to attempt a frontal attack or a midnight break-in. With such a difficult assignment, the ninja would fall back on cunning by proceeding indirectly.

The ninja would first go to the victim's hometown or the village surrounding his castle, deliberately refraining from contacting him directly. Presenting a letter of introduction to the local priest, he would obtain a position at one of the Buddhist temples or Shinto shrines. Since the family records were kept by shrines and temples in those days, he systematically checked the person's record, learned his personality traits and habits, and found out his personal ties. He might then befriend someone close to the targeted victim, someone who could exert his or her influence. Through this channel, the ninja secured a position in the victim's household. Thus, he gained entrance to the enemy lord's villa or castle through the back door, and when the chance presented itself, the ninja assassinated him.

Another interesting strategem was devised to detect the presence of an enemy ninja in the allied camp. Called *yamabiko shicho no jitsu,* it meant "listening to the echo". The ninja would provide false information directly to the suspected enemy agent and then closely observe his reaction or counteraction. However, the misleading intelligence was usually provided indirectly since it was safer that way and served to hide the true intentions of the allied ninja.

Some important battle plans might be left where the enemy ninja might see them. The date of the attack set for a day or two hence would be included, forcing the ninja, if he were an enemy, to show his hand since he would have to slip out the information as soon as possible. Any suspicious moves on his part, then, would confirm the allied suspicions. The enemy ninja would not necessarily be a double-agent; he might be a spy disguised as a soldier, a laborer or member of the household rather than posing as an allied ninja.

Cloak of Secrecy

The elaborate lengths to which the ninja went to hide his identity and cloak his activities in secrecy can be seen from another tactic called *yomogami no jitsu* - "a hair-do seen from four different views should appear the same". Translated into ninja terms, this meant that the ninja maintained four disguises: two different names and two different personalities. The famous jonin of the Iga School of Ninjitsu, Sandayu Momochi, maintained three separate households, each with its own family.

The unique part of this tactic, however, was the tendency for ninja leaders to operate two separate ninja networks competing against each other. Sandayu (also called by his title "Tanba no Kami"), for example, operated a second band of ninja under the name Nagato Fujibayashi. Amazingly enough, this non-existent jonin and his powerful, and real, group of ninja attained considerable fame for their exploits in vying with the ninja network that operated under Sandayu's own name.

But when the small ninja army fought against Nobunaga Oda's huge forces, Sandayu Momochi at last found it impossible to fight in two different places at the same time and under two different names to keep up the deception. Thus, while Sandayu's name is mentioned for his courageous fighting, Nagato Fujibayashi's name is conspicuously missing from the annals of the battle. From this discrepancy, historians assume that Sandayu Momochi and Nagato Fujibayashi were one and the same man.

One of the main reasons Oda invaded the ninja heartland was because of his bitter enmity toward Buddhist leaders and all their allies, including the Iga ninja. The ninja, having developed from *Yamabushi,* or mountain warrior monks, naturally continued to maintain very close ties with Buddhist priests. Oda was also stirred into action by two assassination attempts on his life, apparently by two Iga ninja. Actually, Sandayu sent the same ninja twice under different names and different disguises.

Obviously, nothing – however minute and seemingly trivial – was overlooked by the ninja. When he donned a disguise as a merchant, for example, and set out on a mission to a new district, he not only had to familiarize himself with the local dialect of that district but was also required to actually learn the ins and outs of being a merchant. *Hengen-kashi no jitsu* is concerned with this phase of ninja activity.

The ninja concentrated on seven main disguises, and although these were expanded on occasion, he normally learned the skills involved with the trade or profession of each type he assumed. There were a monk, a commoner, a Yamabushi, a strolling magician with a monkey, a strolling actor, a merchant and a *komuso,* or itinerant priest. A kakemono scroll painting dating back to the Edo Period (1616-1867) depicts ninja disguised as farmers, priests and even gangsters.

Besides the dialect of a foreign district, the ninja also acquired the manners and customs of the inhabitants. He studied its geography and whatever products it produced. And if the information were available he boned up on the character and background of the district leaders.

The ninja also made it a practice to develop a skill in

DISGUISED as farmers, priests, merchants and even gangsters on this Edo Period (1616-1867) kakemono scroll painting at left, ninja were prepared for combat at all times with such typical weapons as the kusari-gama (shown in upper, right-hand corner). Above, an enemy swordsman has apparently penetrated the disguise of a ninja dressed as a komuso, or itinerant priest, and the ninja must block his blow with a bamboo flute, or shakuhachi.

copying the writing styles and signatures of important enemies, a strategem known as *gisho-giin no jitsu.* Signatures at that time were written within a small square like a seal or a monogram. Thus, the ninja was an accomplished counterfeiter, always collecting the calligraphy and signatures of the enemy at every opportunity.

The Fifth Columnist

The Iga School of Ninjitsu, according to Okuse, trained its ninja in 10 *toiri* tactics – laying the groundwork before war broke out. The ninja was expected to succeed in invading enemy territory to set up a spy ring and ready other strategy in line with the impending conflict.

The first of these tactics was called *katsura-otoko no jitsu,* based on an old Chinese tale about a man in the moon. A ninja operating in enemy territory was called *katsura otoko* because he was almost as isolated as if he were living on the moon. He invariably cultivated a person known as a *chitsumishi* who acted as a supporter for the ninja and allowed his house or shop to be used as a base of operations for the katsura otoko ninja. There is the case of one far-sighted ninja who retained a young married couple and their family living in enemy territory, helping to support them and acting as their patron. Ten years later the investment paid off when the ninja asked the parents to offer their pretty 15-year-old daughter to the enemy warlord. Needless to say, she served as a female ninja spy for him.

The second toiri tactic, *joei no jitsu,* was the dispatch of ninja to enemy territory when hostilities were about to break out. When a region was in the grip of an emergency, it was easier to secure a position. The army was beefed up, more people were needed to do the work involved in launching a war, and since manpower needs were urgent, not too much time was spent investigating the background of applicants. It was all a matter of proper timing for the ninja fifth column to move into enemy territory without creating suspicion.

Utilizing women and turning them into effective female ninja agents was called *kunoichi no jitsu*. These Mata Haris received the same rigorous training as their male counterparts in tactics and strategy. If they were to penetrate the court, they were taught the necessary manners and courtly speech, much as Eliza Doolittle was transformed into a "fair lady" by Professor Higgins in George Bernard Shaw's "Pygmalion". The most beautiful female ninja were earmarked as paramours for enemy warlords. Their objective would either be to pump them for vital information or even assassinate them, if necessary, by stabbing them with their dirks or daggers or their trusty, needle-sharp hairpins.

Most kunoichi were taught how to handle ninja weapons, but if worse came to worse and the female ninja were caught without a weapon, she could momentarily startle her attacker by baring her breasts. If he managed to grab her, she could always crack him against the ears with both hands at the same time and thus break his eardrums. She often took the easy way out by hitting him in his most vulnerable spot, bringing up a sharp knee thrust to the crotch.

There were occasions when the ninja had use of common people living and working in enemy territory. Termed *satobito no jitsu,* in this tactic the ninja ferreted out some commoner or merchant angry with his lord, or with an overweening ambition for success and fame, or an ungovernable desire to acquire wealth. Disgruntled and ambitious citizens have long been obvious targets for secret agents and are still near the top of the list today.

The fifth toiri tactic, *minomushi no jitsu,* means "a worm in the body". This concept resembles somewhat the Western principle that one bad apple can destroy a whole barrel of good apples. The aim was to make enemy subjects or the retainers of an enemy lord the worms in the body by recruiting them into an espionage network and enticing them to betray their own lord. The higher the rank, the more valuable he was to the network.

Hotarubi no jitsu, or firefly glimmer, was a tactic in which a ninja passed through enemy territory carrying a false, confidential message. He allowed himself to be captured so that the message would be discovered and thus mislead the enemy. Another tactic, sounding like a plot for a Hollywood spy film, was called *fukuro-gaeshi no jitsu.* A ninja would pretend to betray his own lord and manage to "escape". After making his way to the enemy lord who had meanwhile learned of his betrayal, the turncoat ninja attempted to gain his trust and serve him as a ninja agent. He might perform some daring or courageous deed to win his confidence. When the battle reached a crisis, the double-agent suddenly betrayed the enemy lord and returned to the allied camp.

It was a dangerous mission, needless to say, for one false move on his part could mean instant death for the ninja. Christopher Plummer in the movie "Triple Cross", a film story that was based on a real experience, served the British in Germany during the war as a double agent. In a variation of this tactic, and one that occurred in the film, the enemy lord could take advantage of the ninja's familiarity with his own home territory by sending him back there as a spy or to carry out an act of sabotage. Consequently, the double-agent ninja could not be well known in his homeland. To keep up the deception he would send back some true but trifling information as well as some important but misleading secrets that were all but impossible to double-check. At the same time, he kept his own allied lord up to date on any information he was able to learn through his communications with the enemy lord. If he were finally able to learn that the enemy was about to attack, plus when and where, he passed the secrets on to his lord and gave up his role as a double agent when the battle began.

A twist of the previous tactic was *tensui no jitsu,* or "spitting at the heavens". In this case, the enemy ninja was the spittle. Once he had been detected, he was provided with harmless bits of intelligence as well as false information.

FEMALE NINJA were trained just as vigorously in the art of self-defense as their male counterparts. Here (near right), an assailant lears through the bushes at a pretty kunoichi walking through the woods. When she comes to an open field (below), the attacker suddenly rushes toward her and tries to force her off her feet (far right, top to bottom). But the seemingly defenseless female counters the attack by slapping both of his ears simultaneously, breaking his eardrums. The attacker is rendered unconscious by the effective blow, and the lovely kunoichi rolls free.

Then, by offering him a better reward, the allied lord persuaded the enemy ninja to swap sides and join the allies. No overt change was made so that the enemy continued to trust him as one of its own agents.

The principle of the relaxed bow, *chikyu no jitsu,* symbolized the ninja as a bow with a loosened string waiting for the day to be restrung and ready for action again. This tactic was used when an allied ninja was captured. Pretending to betray his lord and accepting the offer of the enemy lord to serve as his agent, the captured ninja bided his time until he saw an opportunity to rejoin his own side. Of course, not all captured ninja were given this chance by the enemy lord. Some were imprisoned or put to death.

Delayed Action

The tenth and final toiri tactic cited by Okuse and used in laying the groundwork before fighting broke out was called *yamabiko no jitsu.* The ninja acted as an echo or, more exactly, like a delayed-action bomb since his mission was to wait for a signal from his lord before taking action in the enemy camp. He quit his own camp, pretending to be on bad terms with his lord. After seeking out the enemy camp, he gained the good graces of the enemy lord and served him faithfully without once giving cause for suspicion. Meanwhile, his own lord gave the signal to assassinate the enemy lord or to take some other pre-arranged action and the ninja promptly responded. The signal might be a bonfire at night on a distant hill or the dispatch of another ninja to the enemy camp to pass on the signal, or it could be a brief coded message left at a predetermined place.

The second of the general category of Ninjitsu espionage tactics, *chikairi no jitsu,* was concerned with the infiltration of enemy lines during a battle. In such cases, the ninja acted in a role similar to that of the famed British commandos of World War II or the Green Berets of the Vietnam War, sneaking behind enemy lines to disrupt his position in guerrilla-like tactics. Okuse mentions eight "strategies for certain victory".

In *ryakuhon no jitsu* the ninja slipped into enemy territory and pretended to be a friend and comrade. However, he had to be already acquainted with key enemy leaders, know the location of enemy houses and possess an intimate knowledge of enemy organization and other data. Once accepted by them as a fellow-warrior, he applied tactics known as *geinyu no jitsu*; this meant discovering the moves of the enemy and taking appropriate counteraction such as demagoguery, haranguing malcontents, and incendiarism, or setting fire to enemy structures. When the enemy forces marched out of their stronghold toward a village, the ninja raced ahead of them to spread panic and confusion among the villagers and thus create an opportunity for stealing the enemy's horses, weapons or food. He also set false rumors afloat and supplied false information to turn the enemy upon himself and cause dissension in the ranks.

Another effective tactic was to take advantage of the enemy's absence from his camp – *katagatae no jitsu*. When the enemy left for a night attack, the ninja slipped into the nearly deserted camp to spy and spread confusion by setting fire to important buildings, powder dumps, armories, warehouses, etc. He also alerted the allied forces for a counterattack against the poorly defended camp. In some cases the ninja hid along the castle wall until an allied attack was launched against the castle at another point. When the defenders rushed to the assaulted part of the castle away from where the ninja was hiding, he took that opportunity to throw his grappling hook atop the wall and quickly pull himself up with his rope. Once inside, he set fires and created as much panic and confusion as possible.

Master of Disguises

Utilizing a tactic known as *yoja no jitsu,* the ninja assumed the appearance of a weak creature to penetrate the enemy's defenses. In other words, he disguised himself as a beggar, a cripple, a madman, a blindman or a deaf mute and stumbled into the enemy camp as part of a rabble, or tagged after merchants.

Creating a diversion was also included among the ninja tactics listed by Okuse. Called *suigetsu no jitsu,* or "moon in the water", it meant getting the enemy to fall for a trick. A small part of the allied force would be moved nearer to enemy lines as a diversion to draw the enemy's attention and cover the ninja sneaking into his camp to cause havoc.

Of course, diversionary attacks have been employed in battles since ancient times. The Japanese in World War II unsuccessfully made a diversionary attack against the Aleutians to draw attention away from their main thrust at Midway Island. But later in the Philippine campaign, the Japanese used empty aircraft carriers to draw away Adm. Bull Halsey's main naval forces while they launched their primary assault against virtually defenseless transports unloading men and supplies off the beaches in Leyte Gulf. Halsey fell for the bait, but a major U.S. disaster was averted by a gallant defense by a handful of U.S. converted carriers and destroyer-escorts plus Japanese timidity at the "moment of truth".

A tactic termed *taniiri no jitsu* was based on the same principle as *yamabiko no jitsu* – mountain echo. The only difference was that a ninja team rather than an individual ninja pretended to betray its lord and switched sides. Then, at a signal from its own lord the team moved into action. In *ryohan no jitsu* the ninja would capture an important official and use him as a hostage. Then, the enemy would be threatened that unless he acted according to instructions the hostage would be killed. The higher the kidnapped victim's rank, the better.

The eighth and last chikairi no jitsu tactic used after the start of the battle was *fukuro-gaeshi zen jitsu*. According to Okuse, ninja, discovering that a relative of an enemy lord belonged to a distant clan, gave the relative a false message from the enemy lord and then promised to carry the reply back to the lord personally. The ninja, of course, had no such intentions. He read the reply, then composed a false letter to the enemy lord. The ninja thus read the actual letters by both sides, but always provided them with his own false versions, continuing the correspondence until the relative was convinced of the "truth" of the false information imparted by the ninja. As a result, the ninja not only learned of the enemy's plans but hopefully converted the relative into spying for him by creating dissension between the relative and the enemy lord.

Penetration

The ninja devised five basic techniques for breaking into the enemy camp, according to Okuse. The first, *nyukyo no jitsu,* or invasion, meant that the ninja always went to special pains to select the proper timing for entering the enemy camp; for example, when most of the enemy's forces were away fighting somewhere, or the first couple of days after setting up camp. In the latter instance the ninja took advantage of the fact that the enemy didn't get properly organized until after a few days. Another opportune time to sneak into the enemy stronghold was on the night the enemy arrived from a long, tedious journey or the night following a day-long battle.

Other timely moments for slipping through enemy defenses coincided with cooking and mealtimes, taking care of the horses, getting ready to bed down for the night or preparing for a night raid or early-morning attack. Choice times were also the night after the enemy launched a successful night attack or after he had won a battle since he would be exuding confidence and therefore would be relaxed, his guard down. A night when a strong wind was blowing was also propitious for invading the camp as well as a rainy, snowy, foggy or moonless night or

BREAKING AND ENTERING was the ninja's special talent, whether the object of penetration was a castle, a locked room or chest. At left, a ninja disguised beneath a basket hat battles with a ninja guard at the entrance of a castle. Ninja were masters at penetrating enemy strongholds, but attempts were usually made at night when chance for detection was less. Expert burglars, ninja used a variety of tools, above, for breaking-in tactics. Once in, the ninja lay his obi, below, across the floor and silently tread along its narrow width.

just after a serious accident had occurred in the camp. By the same token, the ninja would refrain, whenever possible, from making any attempt at entering the enemy camp on ordinary moonlit nights or when the enemy was expecting an attack and was therefore on special alert. A time of activity was also preferred to a period of quiet.

The best time for a ninja to sneak into the villa compound or house of an enemy lord would be the night after some special daytime ceremony such as a wedding or a birthday, the night after a member of the family had recovered from an illness, just after a serious accident or a family death, a stormy night or a night when a fire or some unusual accident had occurred near the house.

Discovering a weak place in the defense of the camp, castle or villa of the enemy was called *monomi no jitsu*. The ideal place would be on the opposite side of any busy place such as a kitchen, dining room or storeroom. The ninja aimed at breaking into the back entrance, an empty room, an empty guest room or toilet. The same principle would be applied when trying to sneak into an enemy encampment or castle.

Blind Spot

Another tactic used in sneaking into the enemy camp was for the ninja to take advantage of a weak or blind spot in the psychological makeup of a guard - *nyudaki no jitsu*. The "da" in nyudaki means "idleness" and "ki" means "a dislike for being industrious". A ninja thus attempted to discover a guard's shortcomings: laziness, stupidity, etc. A similar tactic, called *yoji-gakure no jitsu,* symbolically used a toothpick. The ninja approached a guard from the rear and threw a *yoji,* or toothpick, over his head to draw his attention. When the guard went to examine the slight noise, the ninja slipped past him.

Actually, the ninja used any small object to distract a guard's attention, such as a pebble or tiny metal sliver. But such a simple trick couldn't be pulled on an ordinary guard; the ninja had to know that the guard was either lazy, dull-witted or drunk. Moreover, the ninja didn't always throw the distracting object over the guard's head; rather, he might toss it to one side or the other, depending on circumstances and the physical layout of the gate or door where the guard was stationed.

In being aware of the best chance for taking action, the ninja kept three taboos in mind: never look down on the enemy and underestimate his abilities; never be afraid of the enemy and act with a lack of self-confidence; never hesitate to take action when that is the most effective way to achieve one's aims.

The thoroughness of a ninja's training is also shown by *joei-on jitsu,* the erasing of sound and shadow. He always moved behind the light source to keep from casting a shadow. In case watchdogs were kept by the enemy to guard their camp or villa, the ninja made sure he moved to the leeward, or downwind, so that his scent would not be carried back to the dog which was the most feared enemy used in detecting a ninja. To keep from making sounds, the ninja wore cotton padding in his sandals or tabi and kept away from straw or bamboo which made a rustling sound that a dog or guard could detect.

Another interesting result of the ninja's training was his ability to judge the depth of a person's sleep, which was extremely important while sneaking into a castle or villa on special night missions, whether for eavesdropping, stealing a valuable document or assassinating an enemy general or warlord. This judgement was based on the age and size of the person as well as the season of the year and the time of the night.

For instance, the ninja chose spring and summer seasons for sneak attacks since he found people grew sleepy early in spring and slept deeply after midnight in summer, tired out by the day's heat. He also knew that older people slept fewer hours, fat people generally slept well and thin persons lightly. He also had to be careful in autumn and winter because people are less tired during these seasons and their sleep is comparatively lighter. In addition, the ninja observed the breathing and snoring so that he could distinguish between pretended and real sleeping. Ninja learned that real snoring has an irregular sequence while false snoring has a regular sequence of breathing noises.

Tricks

It goes without saying that when worse came to worse the ninja always had a trick or two up his sleeve that would enable him to deceive his enemy. Many of these tricks were used in eluding guards and penetrating enemy strongholds. Since the people in those days were very superstitious, it was only natural that the ninja take advantage of their fears with a trick called *kyonin no jitsu*.

For example, it was a popular superstition that the big gate in the Iga Hachiman Shrine, in what is now Okazaki City, Aichi Prefecture, invariably moved before an accident or disaster occurred. One day the gate moved, causing the people to fear they might be attacked. As a result, they began making hurried preparations for war, bolstering their stocks of weapons and food. It turned out, however, that Ieyasu Tokugawa, shogun at the time, had his Iga ninja under Hanzo Hattori frighten the people into concentrating their efforts on preparedness by secretly slipping inside the big gate and moving it when the area was full of people.

Ametori no jitsu was a trick based symbolically on the old belief that birds don't fly on rainy nights. Okuse tells of how the famous Japanese general and unifier of Japan, Hideyoshi Toyotomi, adapted an idea from this trick when he was still a low-ranked samurai. He bet a friend that he could steal his sword within 10 days. Of course, his friend was on the alert all the time. On the seventh night it rained and he heard the sound of a rubber raincoat flapping softly in the garden like the wings of a bird. Immediately, he smiled to himself as he guessed that Hideyoshi was making an attempt to steal the sword. He opened the sliding door and went outside, but found only a stone lantern covered by the raincoat. Hideyoshi wasn't there. Suddenly aware of the fact that he was being tricked, he rushed back into the house only to find the sword was gone. Hideyoshi had taken advantage of the idea that a raincoat always indicated the presence of a man inside it.

On Cat's Feet

When the ninja attempted to slip near the sleeping enemy and observe his depth of sleep, he sometimes imitated the sound of a cat, rat, or similar small animal in order to cover any noise he might make and put the enemy's subconscious mind at rest with a natural sound.

If the ninja were on the point of being discovered by the enemy while sneaking into his stronghold, he sometimes made the sound of a common animal such as a dog, cat or rat. Or he might suddenly speak out in a loud voice, pretending to be one of the enemy. When he was actually discovered, he would pretend to escape by running a few steps in the darkness. But he would suddenly stop and throw some object far off to draw the enemy's attention that way, then silently slip off in another direction. This trick was especially useful when the ninja had still not reached his destination and simply wanted to throw the enemy off his track long enough for him to continue on his way and complete his mission.

A trick called *ennyu no jitsu* was used to break into a heavily guarded castle, according to Okuse. Making sure that the enemy detected his actions, the ninja would pretend to aim at the back gate. While drawing attention to the rear gate, the ninja really intended to slip through the front gate. A similar trick was to design two simultaneous activities, one a feint, or diversion, and the other his real intent.

In the event a ninja was captured and tied, he used a trick called *nawanuke no jitsu,* the technique of loosening a knot or escaping from the bonds by dislocating his joints or keeping some tiny object in his hand to cut the cords. Manipulation of the joints was one of the first things a young ninja learned. He was also adept at concealing a small blade or cutting tool in his hand, between his toes, in his ear, mouth, etc.

Other ninja tricks were concerned with large-scale actions. *Chakuzen no jitsu,* for instance, provided that a ninja hid himself in a loft, ceiling, attic, storeroom or under a passageway before fighting broke out and waited for the battle to begin, for days at a time if necessary. He then emerged to create as much upheaval and confusion in the enemy camp as possible. *Hoka no jitsu* involved setting fire to structures inside the enemy stronghold when a battle erupted, thus compounding the panic. The ninja's three main tasks at this time were to set fires at many different places in the enemy camp, to spread false rumors and try to cause panic among the soldiers, and to open the enemy gates to the allied army.

When a three-man ninja team planned to penetrate or escape from an enemy camp, the top man went first and the No. 2 man brought up the rear, all three proceeding at specified intervals, not in a bunch. One of the most common ways to enter the enemy camp was for the ninja to disguise himself as a common foot soldier in the enemy army. Since they all wore the same uniform and there were so many of them, it was difficult to detect a disguised ninja among their midst.

The Invisible Man

Inpo, the art of hiding, was an integral part of the ninja's skills. He took advantage of every possible object, natural as well as man-made, to conceal himself from the enemy. In fact, his ability to hide himself so completely was what gave rise to the legends that ninja could make themselves invisible at will. He would blend in with and become part of a tree, stone lantern, wall, fence or hedge. Since he was a master at controlled breathing techniques, he was able to remain motionless for long periods at a time. He also covered his face and closed his eyes, concentrating on hearing.

Uzura gakure no jitsu involved hiding like a quail *(uzura)* in small gaps between two larger objects such as the gap between two trees, a rock and grass, a tree and a rock, etc. The ninja would bend over double, making himself into a squarish object. He could assume a rectangular shape by standing erect with his legs together, arms at his sides and his head bent down onto his chest. Depending on the size and shape of the gap to be filled, he would convert himself into that particular shape.

Another technique noted by Okuse called for the ninja to

hide in grass or bushes, but not on windy days when sound carries further. He was also careful not to walk on dry leaves. There was even a technique for hiding in the shadows of trees, garden stones, stone lanterns, etc. At the same time he was careful not to look out a window with the light at his back when sneaking around an enemy villa.

Tanuki gakure no jitsu referred to raccoons and meant that the ninja should be able to climb a tree like a raccoon and press himself as close as possible to the trunk or a thick branch so that he should seem part of the tree. *Kitsune gakure no jitsu* was imitating the actions of a fox in hiding himself in water. The ninja covered his face with duck weed or reeds and, if necessary, sank below the surface and breathed through a reed.

In *shiba gakure no jitsu* the ninja made use of piled-up objects such as lumber, charcoal bags, straw rice sacks, etc. He simply hid himself among these objects so that it would be virtually impossible to detect him at a casual glance. Of course, he would usually bury himself out of sight among the objects piled up. When an emergency arose and he had to conceal himself in a hurry, the ninja sometimes jumped into an empty cask, box or straw bag, but such hiding places were too obvious if his presence were known and he were being chased. He also hid himself in empty chests so that the enemy would unwittingly carry him deep into a castle.

When hiding under corridors or passageways, the ninja camouflaged his head and part of his body with bamboo branches and leaves. But when the ninja hid under floors or in attics, he had to be on the alert for probing swords and spears. Many suspicious samurai in those days made it a routine practice when they entered a room for the first time to jab their swords and spears through the tatami floor or into the ceiling to check for eavesdropping ninja concealed there. When a sword blade came whistling past his nose or through part of his clothing, the ninja had to remain absolutely still so as not to give himself away. Of course, if the blade cut through his flesh, the blood on the steel would betray his presence even if he clenched his teeth and didn't cry out. Movie makers are fond of showing a samurai jabbing a spear into the ceiling and then a few seconds later, have blood dripping down.

Tonpo, or escape techniques, were vital to the success of any mission since capture could possibly undo everything. And like every other phase of ninja activity, nothing was overlooked that might assist him. He made the most of atmospheric conditions, for example, in which to escape: blinding sunlight, deceptive moonlight, thunder, lightning, wind, clouds, rain and even snow. The old trick of using a mirror to reflect the sunlight into the enemy's eyes in order to temporarily blind him was included among the ninja's many ruses. Moonlight created an endless variety of shadows in which the ninja could hide long enough during his escape to throw off his pursuers. Fresh, falling snow quickly obliterated his tracks; heavy rain not only discouraged pursuit but also covered the sight and sound of his escape, while clouds passing across the moon would plunge the surrounding scene into sudden darkness and allow the ninja to elude the enemy.

Chiton jitsu, according to Okuse, provided the ninja with the use of water, fire, wood, earth and metal to aid his escape. When available, hot water could be thrown in a pursuer's face as a blinder, or water could be tossed on a fire so that the resultant explosion would startle the enemy and the steam would provide cover for a few precious seconds, allowing him to disappear. Even the sound of water was used. A ninja hiding near a castle moat, a pond or river would throw a stone into the water as far away from his position as possible in order to attract the attention of his pursuers toward that direction.

Fire was also useful to the ninja in escaping. Suddenly stirring up a fire could throw up sparks and flames that would dazzle the enemy, or a piece of burning wood could either be thrown at him or wielded as a weapon. A sudden bright light in the darkness produced by one of the ninja's flashing bombs could momentarily blind a pursuer.

In a field the ninja could set fire to the grass, provided the wind was blowing toward the enemy. If not, he could always circle around to the windward side of his pursuers. As in the case of water, the ninja also made use of sounds from fire. For example, he would throw some chestnuts or pieces of bamboo into a fireplace or bonfire so that when they burned they would explode in a loud popping sound like a gun, sending the enemy scurrying for cover in the belief it was

TO DISCONCERT his attackers, a ninja wears a devil's mask, hoping it will startle them long enough for him to escape. At left, a ninja blends in with a tree in order to hide from his enemies. His ability to merge with the surrounding scenery was what gave rise to stories that ninja could make themselves invisible at will.

CORNERED by his pursuers, a ninja prepares to climb a wall. If his escape were not fast enough for the enemy, the ninja could always throw out a few tetsu-bishi, below, in their path. One step on these vicious little caltrops would be enough to persuade the enemy to give up the chase.

being fired upon. Smoke, of course, provided the best screen for the movements of an escaping ninja. Realizing that a fire was not always handy, he usually carried his own smoke grenades and flash bombs for emergency use.

Wood was helpful, too, although to a lesser extent. Chips of wood or bamboo were used as blinders and thrown into the eyes of an adversary. A piece of wood could also be thrown into a distant bush to distract the ninja's pursuers, and as a last resort a heavy stick could be used like a club for clobbering his enemy on the head or a long, pointed stick would be helpful in keeping a pursuer at bay by jabbing at him when no other weapon was available.

Using the earth to his advantage involved throwing dirt or sand into a pursuer's eyes as a blinder, crashing a big rock over his head or using pebbles and rocks to distract the enemy's attention during a search for an escaping ninja. The ninja also dug holes in advance and then retraced his steps over the same trail during his escape so that he could use the camouflaged hole to hide in or to entrap his unsuspecting enemy.

In a more intricate strategem, the ninja would dig two holes seven or eight feet deep and a few feet apart. Connected at the bottom to allow a fuse to pass between the two holes, the front hole would contain explosives and would be perfectly camouflaged. Then, when he was being pursued, the ninja would leap into the second hole and light the fuse so that as his pursuers ran toward him they would plunge unexpectedly into the front hole and seconds later be blown sky-high by the explosives.

A Sharp Distraction

The ninja used metal in much the same way as the other four elements. Of course, he always carried a supply of multi-pointed shuriken for throwing at the enemy, more to distract him or force him to dodge the attack than to seriously wound him, although a well-aimed shuriken striking a sword-wielding adversary on his hand or arm could temporarily put him out of action. And if it hit him in the eye, it could actually do irreparable damage.

Spiked *tetsu-bishi,* or caltrops, were another ninja favorite for delaying pursuers during an escape. He strewed his line of retreat with them so that when an enemy stepped on one it was usually enough to make him give up the chase. They were designed so that no matter how they landed, one metal spike always pointed upward and could easily pierce the thickest sandal or tabi.

If no shuriken or tetsu-bishi were available, the ninja used metal coins instead as a blinder. Metal statues or large metal vases and other heavy metal objects could also be turned to the ninja's favor, either as weapons or obstacles. For instance, a heavy bronze statue could be pushed over onto a group of pursuers, or a metal vase could be rolled down the stairs being climbed by the enemy. Metal candlestick holders made potent weapons, too. A small metal coin or similar metalic object when thrown against stone made a clinking sound that served to distract the enemy hunting for a hidden ninja.

Making a big hullabaloo sometimes helped the ninja escape. He might make it all the way to the main gate or guardhouse without being discovered, but had to devise some way of outwitting his enemy there to complete his escape. Thus, he would rush up to the guards on duty, and in an excited voice describe a big accident that he claimed had just occurred inside the castle or villa. Constantly looking back and pointing toward the supposed scene of the accident, he would use all of his dramatic technique to convince the guards of the authenticity of the mishap and do his best to get them excited, too. Then in the midst of all this hullabaloo, he would calmly walk out through the main gate, shouting back a final word of warning to be careful.

One of the wittiest strategems employed by the ninja in making good his escape was his use of various small animals and insects: snakes, spiders, centipedes, rats, toads, foxes, monkeys, raccoons, dogs, etc. Chased by guards in a castle or villa, a ninja might pull a snake or scorpion out of his pocket and toss it at his pursuers, startling them for an instant. An instant was all a ninja needed to escape.

Even the age-old trick of suddenly stopping and forcing his closely-pursuing enemy to fall over him was used by the quick-thinking ninja. He would then jump up and quickly run back the way he had just come to confuse his enemy. He also used dogs and monkeys to attack and bite the enemy. When he slipped into an enemy camp, he kept his dog outside, waiting for his return. When the ninja was escaping, he then set his dog on his pursuers, delaying them long enough to make good his escape.

The Vanishing Breed of Knights Without Armor

Little more than an hour's train ride from Tokyo in drowsy little Noda City along the backwaters of the Boso Peninsula lives one of the more interesting men of Japan. He is Yoshiaki Hatsumi, a modern-day ninja who is keeping alive the teachings of Ninjitsu. Hatsumi lays claim to being the 34th successor to the Togakure School of Ninjitsu in a direct line of master-student relationships that stretch back over a 700-year period. He studied Ninjitsu for 10 years under the tutelage of grand master Toshitsugu Takamatsu who at the age of 82 still lives in Kyoto. Considered one of his country's leading experts on the subject, Hatsumi is one of only a small handful of ninja specialists left who is struggling to keep Ninjitsu from becoming a lost art.

That there are a few such men as Hatsumi around at this late date is surprising in itself. He would seem to be a man who, through some oversight of fate, came along too late. After talking with him one gets the feeling that he would be much more in his element 400 years ago, scaling castle walls under the unsuspecting eyes of the guards or engaging in some other feats of derring-do.

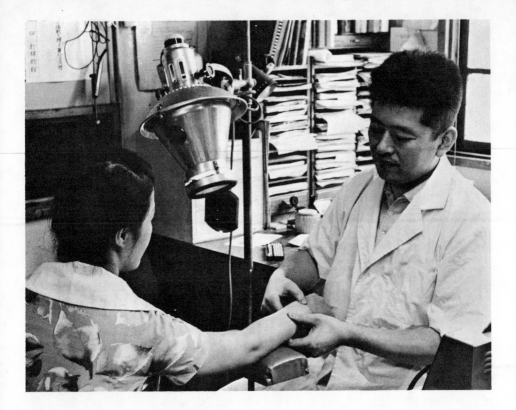

A GRADUATE OF MEIJI UNIVERSITY Medical School, Yoshiaki Hatsumi makes his living at the distinctly unromantic profession of setting broken bones. But precious documents such as the one below give evidence of the scholar's status as the 34th successor to the Togakure School of Ninjitsu that stretches back over a 700-year period.

150

151

NINJA

Madison Avenue Spies

Instead, Hatsumi is a man of the 20th Century, a time when the "romantic adventures" of individual undercover agents are largely eclipsed by the massive and organized efforts of teams of scholarly espionage agents who sit at desks in large office buildings poring over documents to get their information. They have never sneaked into an enemy camp in their lives.

A graduate of Meiji University Medical School and now in his middle 30s, Hatsumi works out regularly at his Ninjitsu dojo to stay in top physical condition. Eating unpolished rice, soybean paste soup and other plant protein also keeps him in trim and gives him plenty of stamina. He doesn't smoke or drink. He also takes a cold shower every morning and exercises vigorously before practice at his dojo. Like ninja of old, he walks on ice with wooden clogs every chance he gets to attain perfect waist balance and to learn to walk in silence.

It was much more exciting in the days when the ninja flourished, however. Hatsumi, for instance, makes his living in the distinctly unromantic profession of setting broken bones. But if things aren't quite so peppy as they used to be, Hatsumi and his fellow ninja of today are at least able to make a decent living. Today's few remaining masters of the art have been able to supplement their incomes by writing books on Ninjitsu and acting as consultants to the television serials and movies that have flourished as part of the ninja craze that has swept Japan the past few years.

During the height of the ninja fad a ninja museum where ninja relics are shown to the public was set up in Iga-Ueno. Foreign tourists have even stopped there and watched ninja expert Heishichiro Okuse, who is also mayor of the city, demonstrate typical ninja techniques such as climbing the walls of the nearby Hakuho Castle. The museum is designed like a typical ninja house, which was invariably disguised as a farmhouse. Such houses were full of trapdoors, secret sliding panels, escape tunnels, etc. Today the city of Iga-Ueno, the former center of Iga ninja activities, is a city of 60,000 persons specializing in the production of string for kimono obi and fish breeding.

FULL OF TRAPDOORS and secret exits, this ninja house, above, now serves as a ninja museum in Iga-Ueno. The entrance to the museum, at right, beckons guests to roam through rooms filled with ninja relics and weapons.

153

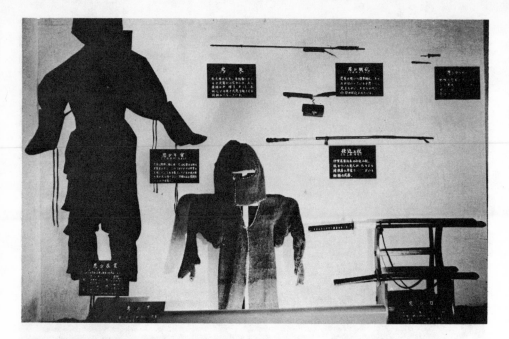

SUIT OF MAIL worn by the ninja is similar to that used to protect the European knights of old. Below, a ninja trio seems prepared for a little night action with, from left, a sword, a dual-purpose ladder and hooking device, and a knotted rope weighted for scaling walls.

DISGUISED AS FARMHOUSES, ninja homes were full of trap doors, secret sliding panels and escape tunnels. A caretaker at the Iga-Ueno Museum demonstrates how attics were rigged with rope ladders so that ninja could make quick exits, if necessary.

MODERN-DAY ninja practitioner Norihiro Iga-Hakuyusai, at left, believes that a ninja must keep himself as sharp as a knife's edge. Heishichiro Okuse, below, is probably Japan's leading scholar and historian on the subject of Ninjitsu and now serves as mayor of Iga-Ueno, the heartland of Ninjitsu.

Southwest of Osaka along the Inland Sea in the city of Himeji stands the stately Himeji Castle. Once a stronghold of Ninjitsu training during feudal times, it is preserved today as a national monument.

The remarkable 72-year-old farmer who used homemade "water shoes" for crossing the three-mile-wide Akashi Strait a few years ago quite possibly learned how to make and use this device from neighboring ninja descendants. But the youth who was caught trying to sneak into the old Imperial Palace in Kyoto undoubtedly learned his ninja know-how from seeing movies and reading magazines. In fact, he told police that he was crazy about the ninja exploits depicted in films and had for a long time wanted to become a ninja himself.

Stories of ninja exploits are usually based on fact, but the details are often only the imagination of the writer or raconteur. Now that new attention has been focused on Ninjitsu, fanciful ninja tales have sprung up everywhere, such as those by Futaro Yamada. This Japanese novelist concentrates exclusively on sex-angled stories of kunoichi, or female ninja, to a point where the reader might be led to believe that most of the feudal-age secret agents were women. Actually, female ninja usually appeared on the periphery of Ninjitsu activities.

Flying Ninja

Ninja adventure stories for boys in the past few years have also been exaggerated out of all proportion to the truth. For example, they tell of flying ninja with skin-and-bamboo wings strapped on their backs being hurled into the air by the snapback from rubbery trees or bamboo stalks lashed together. Other stories depict ninja soaring aloft on huge, two-man kites made of oil-coated paper and bamboo. When the kite drifted over an enemy castle, the ninja tossed down small hand explosives. The kites were controlled by not one, but many strings, and were equipped with blades to cut the strings of enemy kites.

These boys' books would have the reader believe that ninja assaulted castle walls, not with ordinary ladders, but with unique scaling ladders shaped like an "X" and erected atop large framework towers. With ninja clinging to each of the four sections, the X-like ladder revolved much as a windmill turned. As each section swept down past the top of the castle wall, the ninja would leap down, swords in hand, on their enemies.

Another seige device, similar to one that was actually used by Hideyoshi Toyotomi in his invasion of Korea, was a battering ram. Consisting of a huge beam sharpened on the business-end and set up on wheels, it was pulled back and then suddenly released so that it would smash against the enemy's gate and break it. Sometimes a massive rock was used. Suspended by rope from an overhead cross beam, the rock was hauled back and then let go to slam against the gate.

One of the most original devices was a kind of tank which if it had been employed by ninja would have been extremely effective. Two giant wooden wheels with iron rims were set up on either side of a fortified wooden section at the center which was hung loosely on the axel so that it didn't turn around with the wheels. This center section had room for four ninja: two bowmen in the open part at the top and two ninja with guns projecting through slits in the middle. Some experts claim that a contraption like this was actually used when the allied army which the ninja was fighting for held the high ground. The wheeled devices were rolled down the hill pell-mell, with the ninja blazing away and the "tank" running down anyone who stood in the way.

Human Cannonballs

An incredible aerial maneuver was designed to shoot ninja out of such powerful cannons that the blast would send them sailing over the enemy position until they made a soft landing on the other side by parachuting down with their capes. Of course, while they flew over enemy territory they dropped grenades and devices filled with explosive powder. Although ninja have been known to break their fall from a great height with their capes, it seems to be stretching things a bit to say that they performed like human cannonballs, sailing over several hundreds of yards and landing without injury.

Ninja were also busy aquatic agents. Long before Captain Nemo came up with his Nautilus (in Jules Verne's "20,000 Leagues Under the Sea"), ninja were supposed to have used wooden, paddle-wheel submarines. They were weighted to sink beneath the waves, and when ready to rise to the surface again, the weights were simply removed. While unseen underwater, the submarines disgorged ninja clad like feudal-age frogmen, forerunners of the scuba agents in the James Bond thriller "Thunderball". Wearing rudimentary goggles and carrying waterproof explosives, the ninja would swim over to attack enemy ships in the harbor or the ocean area in which they were operating.

Famed ninja leader Hanzo Hattori was said to have built a special ship that, instead of using a paddle-wheel, was equipped with a huge, circular blade with sharp, saw teeth. When a submarine was detected, Hattori's ship streaked to the spot and sliced up the ninja enemy's wooden sub with its whirring sea buzz saw.

Of course, not all of these ninja adventure stories for boys should be taken at face value, but here and there they do provide a clue to the way the inventive ninja operated. Moreover, some of these fantastic devices were not completely beyond the realm of possibility, such as the battering ram and the windmill scaling device. These uncanny characters regarded nothing as impossible and not only used whatever was at hand to carry out their missions but were remarkably ingenious in coming up with the most surprising stratagems and tactics as well as the most incredible weapons and special devices.

Heishichiro Okuse, the mayor of Iga-Ueno, is probably the foremost authority on Ninjitsu in Japan today. A scholar and historian, he is the author of four books on the subject. In one book he deals with 160 Ninjitsu patterns and their application to present-day life, especially in regard to competitive situations. This includes the determination to win the victory without fail, regarding nothing as impossible, psychologically sizing up an opponent and accurately predicting his future course of action in various life situations.

Okuse's book on the secret thoughts of Ninjitsu put into print the type of things that formerly were passed down only by word of mouth from father to son, master to student. He points out that the ninja applied brainpower scientifically to every problem he encountered. For instance, Okuse relates how one ninja accurately noted his enemy's daily habits and saw that he was fond of strolling in the garden and smelling his flowers. Otherwise, his enemy was too well protected for the ninja to expect any success in an assassination attempt. His solution, then, was to poison one of the flowers so that when the enemy made his usual rounds he inhaled the poisonous scent and died shortly thereafter.

Author, critic and travel writer Jay Gluck tells another tale of ninja ingenuity in hiding two of his female relatives from an invading army during the War of the Imperial Restoration of 1867. When the enemy army seemed to be getting the upper hand, the ninja detached himself from the fighting and retreated long enough to get home to his two relatives who were sure to fare ill if captured. The ninja amazingly enough made them "vanish from the face of the earth" so that a whole rampaging army passed them by and never noticed them. It seems the ninja buried them both up to their noses in sunken manure pots out in the rice fields and then plopped compost straw over their heads.

A Thin Thread

One of the most daring and imaginative assassination attempts was made by famed ninja hero Goemon Ishikawa. After tremendous efforts, he succeeded in sneaking into the attic over the bedroom of the great samurai general Nobunaga Oda. After Nobunaga had retired for the night, Goemon made a small hole in the ceiling just above the general's head. Then, noiselessly he lowered a thin thread until it hung suspended just above the lips of his sleeping victim. Taking out a vial of deadly liquid poison, the ninja sent the poison, drop by drop, down along the thread and into the mouth of Nobunaga. The light-sleeping general, ever alert for such attempts on his life, managed to awaken in time to prevent Goemon from succeeding with his diabolical trick. When ninja networks were later broken up and Goemon was forced to become a robber, Nobunaga's successor, Hideyoshi Toyotomi, captured

HATSUMI SWEEPS a bisento toward his student-opponent. This spear-like weapon with a blade resembling that of a scimitar is part of the ninja technique called kuki shin-ryu.

A SPEAR VARIATION, called kamayari, has a curved metal section near the end for use in hooking an enemy's weapon out of his hands. Here, Hatsumi blocks a sword thrust.

FORCING the sword aside with his kamayari, Hatsumi then hooks it away from his opponent and proceeds to thrust home with the point.

A VIEW OF THE ACTION at Yoshiaki Hatsumi's Ninjitsu dojo shows the teacher, at left, practicing a kicking technique with one of his students who wears a kendo body protector. The power of gyokku-ryu, a series of techniques based on the use of the thumb and fingers as weapons, is evidenced below. The digits can be strengthened to the point where they can deal devastating blows against vital parts of the body.

DAILY PRACTICE toughens Hatsumi's fingers and thumbs as part of gyokko-ryu tactics.

A PADDED POLE supports Hatsumi's blows to toughen his feet. Such exercises help kicking.

PINNING HIM against a wall, a student uses a Y-stick to help Hatsumi with neck-toughening exercises.

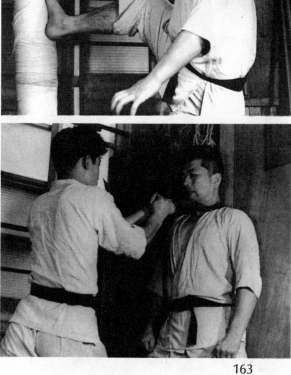

163

YUMIO NAWA has been in-
volved with Ninjitsu for nearly
40 years and is the author
of two books on the subject.

LEADING, present-day
Ninjitsu practitioners
Yoshiaki Hatsumi, left, and
Yumio Nawa are keeping the
art alive.

the daring ninja and executed him by having him thrown into a cauldron of hot, bubbling water.

One of the most remarkable stories of the courage and cleverness of two famous ninja leaders, Sasuke Sarutobi and Hanzo Hattori, is recounted by ninja scholar Okuse. The former ninja was in the employ of Hideyori Toyotomi, Hideyoshi's son, while the latter was allied with Gen. Ieyasu Tokugawa. Following the death of Hideyoshi in 1598, the two clans became deadly enemies in the bitter struggle for power. The Toyotomi forces sent Sasuke from their Osaka Castle headquarters to the district controlled by the Tokugawa army— present-day Aichi Prefecture and Nagoya Castle—to find out if Tokugawa planned to attack them soon.

Tokugawa's ninja bodyguards regularly searched the attics and under the corridors, but Sasuke slipped through the garden. The important meeting of Tokugawa and his aides was held in the general's private rooms, where plans were disclosed to go ahead and assault Toyotomi's castle in Osaka. After overhearing the plans, Sasuke started to leave. He climbed the wall safely, but when he jumped down the other side his left foot got caught in a steel trap. Unable to extricate himself and fearful that the guards would soon find him, the courageous ninja cut off his left leg. He applied a tourniquet to stop the flow of blood, then tried to make good his escape. After dragging himself as far as possible and almost fainting from loss of blood, Sasuke Sarutobi finally committed hara-kiri.

But strange to say, Sasuke continued to appear nightly in the Tokugawa castle, announcing himself and revealing that suicide was merely one of his secret techniques he used to escape from dangerous situations. And every night this remarkable ninja jonin slew a couple of guards. The news of these strange doings soon reached the Toyotomi Clan which was relieved to hear of Sasuke's amazing success, certain that sooner or later he would manage to assassinate Gen. Tokugawa himself.

The Toyotomi forces soon relaxed their guard in overconfidence. Firmly convinced that all was well, they were taken by complete surprise when Tokugawa's army attacked Osaka Castle a few days later and eventually overcame their resistance. It was only later that the nightly appearance of

Sasuke Sarutobi was discovered to be a trick devised by Hanzo Hattori who had disguised himself as his famed rival in order to create a false sense of confidence in the Toyotomi forces. Whether he actually killed some of his own guards to lend the charade a bit of authenticity or whether the reports of their deaths were merely falsified was never revealed. After the final defeat and surrender of the Toyotomi army, Hanzo continued to pass himself off as Sasuke Sarutobi in order to obtain information of the whereabouts of the remaining members of the enemy forces who managed to escape and hide out.

Becoming a ninja in this day and age, however, is a real problem. Norihiro Iga-Hakuyusai, the son of an Iga ninja practitioner, is unmarried, childless and without relatives—an elusive loner. He refuses to divulge any information about himself and maintains no fixed address because, as he says, ninja should always be on the move, never settle in one place and keep themselves out of the limelight. Claiming that a ninja should be like the shadow of a bushi, he has a sponsor because Otomo Saiji, sometimes called Japan's first ninja, operated under the patronage of Prince Shotoku (593-622 A.D.) as a special investigator.

Iga-Hakuyusai started his ninja training at the age of six under the tutelage of his father and during the war taught at Nakano Academy, the former military intelligence school. He notes that the character "nin" in ninja is made up of two parts, one meaning "the spirit of man" and the other meaning "edge". It is this "edge" that should be stressed, he says, for a ninja must keep himself as sharp as a knife's edge. As a modern ninja, Iga-Hakuyusai devotes his time to performing for Japanese school children around the country.

Learning Ninjitsu today as a student, in contrast to being born into an old ninja clan, takes many long years of intense study and dedication. Yoshiaki Hatsumi estimates it takes at least 10 years, the length of time he studied under Takamatsu, to master all the different weapons and techniques: *Fudo-ryu* includes *jujitsu and iainuki,* or fast sword-drawing techniques. *Tegaki yoshin-ryu* takes in *jutai-jitsu.* The third class, or school of techniques, *gyokku-ryu,* includes *yubi* methods (use of thumb and finger) and *Togakure-ryu,* a 700-year-old school emphasizing original ninja techniques. *Koto-ryu* is centered around a technique called *koppo,* or bone breaking. The final school, *kuki shin-ryu,* is based on *bisento,* a type of fighting using a wide-bladed spear with a blade similar to that of a scimitar.

Ninjitsu employs an awesome collection of weapons, but Hatsumi prefers unarmed, self-defense techniques, with koppo his favorite.

"I am best at bone-breaking techniques that can kill with only one finger," he says. These techniques have something in common with karate, though there are differences. For example, blows are always made at 90-degree angles, straight down or straight across. Moreover, the blow is made with the open hand along the bone from the base of the little finger to the end of the palm. But the hand is kept closed in a fist while the arm is in motion, opening only at the instant of contact.

Thumb Power

Another set of techniques that he favors are those for *yubi.* Daily practice strengthens the thumbs and fingers to the point where they can be used to break rocks. Indeed, the thumb can be developed as a powerful weapon against the vital parts of the body, from the eyes to the stomach.

Other ninja have different techniques they specialize in. One modern ninja from Tokyo, for example, who is not too worried about the niceties of the law is Yumio Nawa. Now in his fifties, Nawa has been involved in Ninjitsu for nearly 40 years.

Perhaps Nawa's most outstanding modern ninja technique is one termed *manriki-kusari,* or chain technique. Using a small length of chain less than two feet long, he has devised some 12 basic manriki techniques, all of them defensive. The chain has two small, solid-steel weights at each end which the ninja uses to maintain his grip on the chain as well as for counterblows.

If an attacker swings a right, the ninja first blocks the blow upward with the outstretched chain, then throws a loop around the arm and with the steel block in his right hand counters with a blow under the arm. Another technique is to throw a loop against the attacker's right wrist and pull the other end of the chain around the right side of his neck, pinioning his arm under his own neck. Counterblows with one or both weights can be made against the vital parts of the body such as the temples, neck, solar plexis, etc. The chain can also be used to parry a kick and deliver a telling counterblow with the two weights against the shin before the foot hits its intended target.

Nawa also knows some 40 techniques for tying up an enemy with a rope. Like the chain, these techniques can be applied very usefully today, especially in police and guard work as well as militarily, when tying up guerrilla prisoners, for instance. In fact, Nawa has passed on some of his more practical know-how to the police on several occasions.

These techniques have largely been handed down from ninja days. Since the ninja were trained escape artists, special ways had to be devised to tie them securely. One way was to have them clasp their hands together, then loop the cord around each individual finger before tying the hands together. Ninja often tried to develop their fingers so that their knuckles would not protrude which would prevent effective tying of the fingers.

Ninja also tried to develop their wrists so that the wrist-joint bone wouldn't project beyond the rest of the wrist which would enable the ninja to slip the knot off without too much trouble. They would also roll about the floor or twist this way and that to loosen the knots.

Seiko Fujita, who died at the age of 65, claimed to be a direct descendant of the Koga School of Ninjitsu in the master-student relationship. He was quite vocal in urging Japanese Olympians to adopt ninja techniques for the Games a year before the 1964 Tokyo Olympics were due to open.

Iron Fist

Before he died, Fujita gave many ninja demonstrations around the country, including one in which he beat his chest with a 27-pound iron bar. He claimed ninja could jump as high as 2.7 (8'9") meters compared to the world record

A COLLECTION OF NINJA WEAPONS and devices are displayed by Yumio Nawa in the photo above. In the center is the chain used in manriki-kusari while at right is a weapon similar to kusari-gama—the scythe and chain. Perhaps Nawa's most outstanding modern ninja technique is one termed manriki-kusari, or chain technique. Below, Nawa displays a small length of chain less than two feet long with weights at each end.

A SMALL LENGTH of chain less than two feet long and with weights at each end is proved by Yumio Nawa to be a potent, defensive weapon in manriki-kusari technique. In this instance Nawa blocks a right thrown by his attacker and from this position can easily apply one of several techniques to render his opponent helpless.

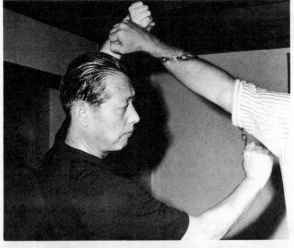

BY LOOPING the chain around his attacker's right arm and holding the steel weight in his right fist, Nawa can then strike a counter-blow under his opponent's arm.

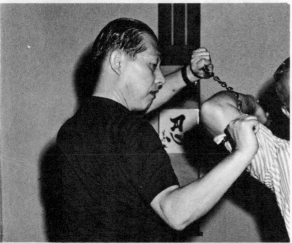

FORCING his attacker off-balance to the rear, Nawa applies two-way pressure — his right arm pulling up, his left arm pulling down.

THE PAIN and pressure of a tightening chain looped just above the wrist puts the attacker at Nawa's mercy.

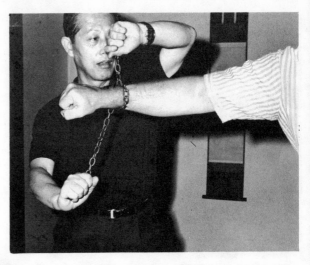

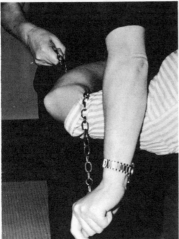

OUT OF COMMISSION, the enemy is forced down toward the floor by Nawa's left-arm power.

IF ATTACKER SWINGS a right, Nawa can throw his chain around the opponent's right wrist, pulling both ends of the chain tightly around the right side of the neck and, in so doing, pinioning the attacker's arm against his own neck.

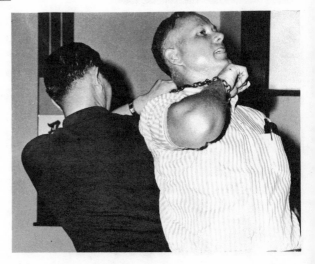

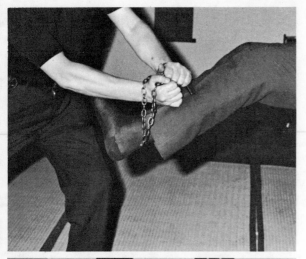

THE CHAIN and two weights can also be used to parry a kick and deliver a telling counter-blow against the enemy's shin before his foot is able to hit its intended target.

SEEMINGLY HELPLESS and unarmed, Nawa is fully prepared for any eventuality with his hands concealing the chain and weights. Counter-blows with one or both solid-steel weights can be made against the vital parts of the body.

STRETCHING the chain behind his back, Nawa finds another way of keeping his weapon concealed but ready for instant use.

at that time of 2.22 (7′3″) meters. Noting that ninja trained night and day to attain their "superhuman" skills, Fujita said they could walk the 350 miles between Osaka and Tokyo in three days.

Hatsumi, who has also studied judo, karate and aikido, has found some of these modern martial arts techniques similar to Ninjitsu methods and has incorporated some of them into his system. For example, if an attacker tries to throw him over his hip, he counters with a sharp blow from the thumb to the side or the kidney before tossing him to the ground.

When an opponent attacks with a right-arm blow, Hatsumi blocks it with his left and counters with his right in a *koppo* blow to break his opponent's right arm. He blocks a kick with a counterkick, then strikes an open-fist blow with his left hand to his rival's ribs and readies another blow from his right hand as the attacker falls.

In one of the most unusual counters Hatsumi will jump on his opponent, straddling his body with both legs, and attempt to crack a few ribs with a leg squeeze. He will then fall backward onto the ground and rock forward again, sending his rival onto his back. He clinches things by slamming a hard blow with his heel into his opponent's face. In a similar maneuver he grabs his rival's midsection and falls backward, pulling him hard onto his head.

Because of his training, Hatsumi has been honored by being the only ninja listed in Japan's official "Martial Arts Directory". Nonetheless, Hatsumi is still critical of government officials for what he feels is their lack of sufficient interest in Ninjitsu.

"I regard Ninjitsu as an intangible cultural asset, despite the indifference of the government," Hatsumi emphasizes. While conceding that Ninjitsu is "extremely dangerous", he believes it is good for self-defense as well as for training both the body and spirit. "By learning Ninjitsu one comes to know how to foresee the future. One finally gets the 'Eyes of God.'"

A Man for All Seasons

What does the feudal-age ninja have to offer contemporary man? Ninjitsu scholar Heishichiro Okuse says their techniques and tactics can be applied to every phase of modern living.

The ninja's passion to excell in everything he undertook as well as his drive for perfection is certainly worthy of emulation. There was no room for mediocrity or dabbling. His whole life, from beginning to end, was dedicated to perfecting his techniques, both from a physical and a mental standpoint. His body, personality and character were honed to a fine point, fitted to the bow of his leader like an arrow and shot straight to his target.

His was a total commitment to the cause of his lord, a loyalty to the death. In a country continually torn by civil strife, who were the bad guys and the good guys? The ninja didn't ponder the ethical aspects of every mission he was assigned to. His loyalty was to his own jonin and it was up to his ninja chief to concern himself with such problems. If his master chose to throw in his lot with a certain warlord, that was good enough for him.

But on a practical basis, what ninja legacy can we make use of today? Both Yumio Nawa and Norihiro Iga-Hakuyusai worked for military intelligence during the war. The art of being a consumate secret agent, of course, is the obvious inheritance handed down by the ninja. Any modern agent would be well-advised to follow his 360-degree approach to every operation, from assuming a disguise, learning the dialect and customs of the region he planned to enter, studying the handwriting of his target and cultivating his victim's close friends to carefully preparing his weapons, special devices, strategy infiltration tactics and final escape route.

The ninja's physical and mental alertness in being ready to make use of anything at hand, no matter how trivial it might seem, to ensure the success of his mission could also be imitated by today's 007s to their advantage. His ingenuity and inventiveness can be seen in the huge array of weapons he employed and the unusual types of special devices he created as well as the incredibly detailed stratagems and tactics he devised.

Sending out two agents on the same mission and secretly setting up rival networks of agents within the same headquarters to provide an in-depth approach to operations are both excellent tactics for intelligence chiefs. Making use of weather conditions for infiltration and penetration, launching surprise attacks and double-checking on one's own agents, from the chief down to the lowest agent (the Philby case should be incentive enough for this procedure) are other easily adaptable and sensible ideas that should be incorporated into modern intelligence activity, if they are not already part of it.

For the budoman or athlete, training methods followed by ninja have a great deal to offer as well as the unarmed combat techniques taught by such men as Hatsumi and Nawa. The latter's chain and rope techniques could also prove valuable additions to one's scope of activities. The Spartan regimen followed by Hatsumi, including his energy-stamina directed diet, is certainly worthwhile testing.

The ninja's ability to read character, predict future behavior and take advantage of an opponent's weaknesses could be applied to any competitive situation, from sports and the martial arts to business and professional activity. Needless to say, this doesn't mean going out and getting your rival drunk or plying him with women in order to defeat him. It can all be done within the mold of contemporary ethics and morality.

Sizing up an opponent in sports and budo, for example, is a virtual necessity. Quickly ferreting out his strengths and weaknesses, and taking advantage of this knowledge, could very well provide the margin of victory when all other things are equal.

If the great ninja of Japan's feudal era were alive today, chances are they would not only turn to military and civilian intelligence, but might turn to industrial spying as well. One can picture them scaling the walls of office buildings, jimmying open the windows and cracking the safe in order to steal some new chemical process. The ninja would have made excellent safe-crackers, among other things.

And if the ninja had bound himself to spy for his country in this day and age, he would have been no summer soldier or sunshine patriot. On the contrary, just as he was in olden times, the ninja would have been a 20th Century man for all seasons.

Glossary

Aisha—A *gojo-gyoku* principle involved with the ninja's manipulation of an overly sympathetic or soft-hearted person.

Ametori no jitsu—A trick taking advantage of the supposition that a raincoat always indicates the presence of a man inside it.

Bisento—Broad-bladed spear.

Bo—Stick.

Bojitsu—Skill with the stick.

Buddhist—One who follows a Central and East Asian religion based on the teachings of Guatama Buddha that Nirvana—escape from suffering and mortality—is the supreme goal attainable and that the way of escape is along the Eightfold Path of right belief, right resolve, right word, right act, right life, right effort, right thinking and right meditation.

Bushido—The way of the samurai; chivalry; military knight ways.

Chakuzen no jitsu—The trick of hiding in a ceiling, attic, etc., of an enemy camp until fighting breaks out, then emerging to cause havoc.

Chikairi no jitsu—Infiltration of enemy lines during a battle.

Chikyu no jitsu—A *Toiri* tactic whereby a captured ninja pretends to betray his own lord until the opportunity arises when he is able to rejoin his own side.

Chiton jitsu—Use of water, fire, wood, earth and metal to aid a ninja in his escape.

Chitsumishi—A citizen of an enemy territory who collaborates with a penetrating ninja.

Chunin—Ninja subleaders.

Daimyo—A feudal lord.

Doka—Pocket heater.

Dosha—A *Gojo-gyoku* concept of taking advantage of man's short temper, inducing him to do something rash.

Ennyu no jitsu—A trick using a feint to get into an enemy camp.

Fudo-ryu—Class of fast sword-drawing techniques.

Fukiya—Pins and poisoned darts shot through blow guns.

Fukumi-bari—Tiny, pin-sized dirks held in the mouth and blown out at the enemy's eyes.

Fukuro-gaeshi no jitsu—A *Toiri* tactic of a ninja supposedly betraying his own lord, "escaping" to an enemy camp, but then betraying the enemy lord at a time of crisis and returning to his allied camp.

Fukuro-gaeshi zen jitsu—A *Chikairi no jitsu* tactic to create dissension between the enemy lord and one of his relatives.

Futokoro-teppo—Bronze pistols.

Geinyu no jitsu—A *Chikairi* tactic whereby a ninja who has secretly penetrated an enemy camp causes havoc by setting fires, etc.

Genin—Ninja agents.

Genmai—Juice made of unpolished rice.

Geta—Wooden sandals (clogs) worn for walking on ice to practice perfect waist balance and silent treading.

Gisho-giin no jitsu—Art of forgery.

Gojo-gyoku—Principle of five feelings and five desires; character flaws.

Gyokku-ryu—Class of techniques—*Yubi*—using the thumb and finger.

Gyokuro—A poison of brewed green tea mixed with *Miso-shiru*.

Hakama—Skirt worn like trousers.

Hengen-kashi no jitsu—The ninja's study and knowledge of each disguise he assumes.

Hoka no jitsu—Setting fires in an enemy camp to spread confusion at the time a battle erupts.

Hotarubi no jitsu—A *Toiri* tactic providing for a ninja to carry a "secret" message through enemy territory so that he will be captured and mislead the enemy with the supposedly confidential information.

Hyakurai-ju—Several small guns set in a circle inside a large, wooden gun barrel; a device mainly used to make a lot of noise.

Iai—The art of drawing a sword.

Iaijitsu—Fast sword draw.

Inpo—The art of hiding.

Jirai—Land mines.

Joei no jitsu—A *Toiri* tactic dispatching ninja to an enemy territory to "serve" in its army when hostilities are about to break out.

Joei-on jitsu—A ninja's training to move without making sound or shadows in order to slip into an enemy camp undetected.

Jonin—Ninja leaders.

Kama—Sickle or scythe.

Kameikada—One-man rafts made with crossed bamboo or timber sections and floated by four large ceramic jars which are sealed so as to be watertight.

Kamigakure no jitsu—"Hiding oneself behind God;" gaining entrance to an enemy lord's castle by befriending one of his associates or relatives.

Katagatae no jitsu—A *Chikairi no jitsu* tactic of spreading confusion in an enemy camp by setting fires, etc., after most of the enemy has left the camp for a night attack.

Katsura-otoko no jitsu—A *Toiri* tactic involving a ninja's operations in enemy territory.

Ken—Sword or blade.

Kenjitsu—Swordsmanship.

Kisha—Taking advantage of an enemy's sensual appetite to bribe him.

Kitsune gakure no jitsu—Technique of imitating the actions of a fox in hiding himself in water.

Komuso—Itinerant priest.

Koppo—Bone-breaking techniques.

Koto-ryu—A class of ninja techniques centered around *koppo*, bone breaking.

Kozutsu—Wooden guns which fire metal balls.

Kuji—The number "nine", the most important number in *Shugendo*.

Kuji-kiri—Hypnotic movement of the fingers.

Kuki shin-ryu—Class of techniques centered around the *Bisento*.

Kumade—A rake usually of four or five long, metal pieces with hooks on the ends extended from a metal ring at the base.

Kumi-uchi—A martial art based on *Sumo* techniques and employed by *samurai* in unarmed combat on the battlefield.

Kunashi—A spade-like, digging device.

Kunoichi—Female ninja agents.

Kunoichi no jitsu—A *Toiri* tactic of training women to be ninja agents.

Kusari—Chain.

Kusari-gama—Skill with the chain and scythe.

Kyobako-fune—A collapsible craft which resembles a wooden chest made waterproof by its fur covering.

Kyoketsu-shogi—A cord, often made of women's hair for extra strength, with a metal ring attached to one end and a double-pointed knife to the other.

Kyonin no jitsu—Taking advantage of one's fears and superstitions.

Kyosha—A *Gojo-gyoku* tactic of handling the cowardly and meek.

Kyujitsu—Archery; skill with bow and arrow.

Manriki-kusari—Chain techniques.

Mikkyo—Esoteric Buddhism.

Minomushi no jitsu—A *Toiri* tactic to get enemy subjects, especially those of high rank, to betray their lord.

Miso-shiru—Soybean paste used in making *miso* soup.

Mizugumo—"Water spider". A water-crossing device consisting of four curved pieces of wood fastened together to form a circle with a hole in the center. A rectangular piece of wood as long as a man's foot is held in the center with cord attached to the circle.

Mizukaki—A web-like device worn on the feet for swimming.

Mizu-taimatsu—A torch designed to burn even during rain.

Monomi no jitsu—Discovering a weak place in the defense of an enemy's camp or castle.

Mugei-mumei no jitsu—The ninja's key to success was anonymity: "No art—no name."

Nawanuke no jitsu—Technique of loosening a knot or escaping from the bonds by dislocating one's joints.

Ninja—A practitioner of the medieval art of *Ninjitsu*; an expert espionage agent.

Ninjitsu—The medieval discipline incorporating the *Bushido* code of the *samurai* as well as every form of martial arts in existence at the time.

Ninshokudai—Candles shaped like the letter "L" so they can be hooked on a wall projection or tree.

Nyudaki no jitsu—Discovering a guard's shortcomings or weaknesses in order to break into an enemy camp.

Nyukyo no jitsu—The technique for proper timing of breaking into an enemy camp.

Omyodo—An ancient, synthetic science which includes the Chinese art of divination and the science of astrology.

Rakusha—A *Gojo-gyoku* principle of tempting a lazy enemy with entertainment.

Ronin—Masterless *samurai*.

Ryakuhon no jitsu—A *Chikairi no jitsu* tactic whereby a ninja slips into enemy territory, pretending to be a comrade.

Ryohan no jitsu—A *Chikairi no jitsu* tactic to kidnap an important enemy official and hold him as a hostage.

Sacchi-jitsu—Military strategy of taking advantage of the natural features of the land.

Sai-min jitsu—An hypnotic art; mesmerism.

Samurai—Warrior.

Sashimi—Raw fish.

Satobito no jitsu—A *Toiri* tactic of instigating dissension among those common people in enemy territory who are already angry or dissatisfied with their lord.

Satsujin-jitsu—Knowledge of atmospheric conditions based on astrology, divination and meteorology.

Shiba gakure no jitsu—Technique of hiding oneself in such objects as lumber, straw rice sacks, etc.

Shikomi-zue—A special sword-cane used by blindmen or those ninja posing as blindmen.

Shinobi-zue—A ninja's staff weapon with a chain hidden in one end and the other end weighted with lead.

Shintoist—A follower of Japan's ethnic cult and religion which shows reverence to the spirits of imperial ancestors and historical personages as well as some deities of nature.

Shochu—Unrefined sake.

Shogun—A military dictator.

Shugendo—Mountain asceticism; a religious campaign proposed in the 7th Century A.D. by a *yamabushi* named En-no-Gyoja to restore order to the nation with a new way of propagating Buddhism.

Shuko—A metal band which slips over the hand, concealing four, sharp spikes on the palm side. (See *Tekagi.*)

Shuriken—Multi-pointed throwing weapons such as dirks and darts.

Suigetsu no jitsu—A *Chikairi no jitsu* tactic of getting an enemy to fall for a trick.

Sumo—Wrestling.

Tabi—Split-toed shoe sock.

Tanagokoro-tai matsu—A small, hand-palm torch.

Taniiri no jitsu—The same tactic as *Yamabiko no jitsu* except a **team** of ninja pretend to betray their own lord and join the enemy's side, rather than an individual ninja.

Tanuki gakure no jitsu—The technique of climbing a tree like a raccoon.

Tekagi—A hook worn like a *Shuko*, useful for gripping when climbing walls, trees, etc., and also used as a weapon to rake an enemy's face.

Tensui no jitsu—A *Toiri* tactic of furnishing an enemy ninja acting as a double-agent with harmless bits of information, then persuading him to work for the allied forces without the knowledge of the enemy lord.

Tetsu-bishi—Four-pointed caltrops.

Tofu—Soft curd made of soybeans.

Togakure-ryu—Hand-to-hand combat technique in which the ninja simultaneously slaps both ears of his rival.

Toiri tactics—Preparing strategy for war.

Tonki—Small metal weapons such as dirks, daggers and darts.

Tonpo—Escape techniques.

Torinoko—Firecrackers shaped like eggs.

Tsune no mizu — Food made from *Umeboshi*.

Ukidaru — Water-crossing devices (floating pots) of waterproof reed pots for the feet used with fan-like, bamboo oars.

Umeboshi — Pickled plums.

Uzura gakure no jitsu — Hiding like a quail in small gaps between two larger objects.

Yagen — Pharmacy; a chemist's mortar.

Yamabiko no jitsu — A *Toiri* tactic in which a ninja supposedly leaves his own camp, on bad terms with his lord, and joins the enemy lord, serving him "faithfully" until the ninja is given a signal to assassinate him or take some other course of action.

Yamabiko shicho no jitsu — "Listening to the echo." A device for detecting a double-agent by providing him with false information and observing his reaction.

Yamabushi — A mountain, warrior priest.

Yari — A spear.

Yarijitsu — Skill with the spear.

Yoja no jitsu — A *Chikairi no jitsu* tactic of penetrating an enemy's defenses by pretending to be a weak person such as a beggar, cripple or blindman.

Yoji — Toothpick.

Yoji-gakure no jitsu — Distracting a guard's attention by throwing a toothpick or pebble over his head in order to sneak into an enemy camp.

Yomogami no jitsu — The ninja's measures to remain anonymous by maintaining two different names and two distinct personalities.

Yubi — A sharp blow with the thumb to an enemy's right kidney.

Zagarashi-yaku — A poison made of green plum or peach.

Zen — A Buddhist sect that believes the way to enlightenment is through meditation, in the traditional lotus position, on nothingness.

Index